by Brian T. Jones, CFP®

Published by:
Larstan Publishing Inc.
10604 Outpost Dr., N. Potomac, MD 20878
240-396-0007 ext. 901
www.larstan.com

PRINTED IN THE UNITED STATES OF AMERICA

10 9 8 7 6 5 4 3 2 1

Design by Rob Hudgins & 5050Design.com
Cover design by Mike Gibson
ISBN, Print Edition 978-0-9776895-4-5
Library of Congress Control Number: 2006930835
First Edition

CRITICS AGREE...GETTING STARTED: THE FINANCIAL GUIDE FOR A YOUNGER GENERATION IS A HIT!

"Living within the professional football world we see too many young men and women who according to Jones, 'allow themselves to live a lifestyle that is simply beyond what their cash flow will support.' This step-by-step tutorial uses humor to analyze the psychology of spending, which helps readers understand how they, too, might be defining their worth by material possessions.

With vivid examples of real-life couples from all backgrounds, the typically lackluster topics of social security, taxes and insurance coverage are covered with zest. Jones proves how aggressive vigilance on all matters financial will either make or break couples as he details the importance of people taking action to protect themselves and their families.

Especially valuable throughout the text are the 'to do lists', the up-to-date toll-free phone numbers and the informational websites so readers can immediately start game planning their financial future.

Even for those who are debt-free and financially comfortable, this book serves as a refreshing reminder that as life changes so should the financial focus."

Shannon O'Toole – author of
Wedded to the Game: the Real Lives of NFL Women
John Morton – Passing Game Assistant, New Orleans Saints (NFL)

"As a financial professional who has advised thousands of people of all ages on their financial needs and concerns, I have seen first hand how confused they are about the simplest—and most complex—financial concepts. As the national president for the country's largest social fraternity, I am approached everyday by college men who are looking for a resource they can turn to that will help answer their financial questions. In both roles I have seen the need for a book like *Getting Started: The Financial Guide For A Younger Generation*. It is a book that will help people of all ages."

J. Michael Scarborough, Author of The Scarborough Plan: Maximizing the Power of Your 401(k), *President of The Scarborough Group, and National President of the Sigma Alpha Epsilon Fraternity*

"I am often asked by clients for a book they can give to their young adult children and grandchildren as they embark into life after college. "Getting Started" is the perfect solution as it gives practical financial planning advice for Generation Xers written by a Generation X financial planner who speaks their language!"

Alexandra Armstrong, CFP, Coauthor of On Your Own: A Widow's Passage to Financial and Emotional Well-Being *and Past Chairman of the International Association for Financial Planning (IAFP)*

"As consultants and coaches to financial professionals across the country, we see first hand how advisors struggle to communicate effectively with those in younger generations. Not only are the jargon and strategies complicated to understand, but the ways in which older advisors communicate with younger people does not always work. Brian Jones, CFP, has written a book that will resonate with a younger generation and will serve as a blueprint for others in the industry in their quest to communicate effectively. The future of America depends on them!"

Katherine and Peter Vessenes, Founders of Vestment Advisors, Inc. and Coauthors of the book Building Your Multi-Million Dollar Practice

TABLE OF CONTENTS

GETTING STARTED

It can be difficult to ponder when you're just starting out, but the sooner you can accumulate your pile of wealth, the sooner you can retire to the tropics or just enjoy a slower pace.

We all know accidents happen. But do you know how to minimize the financial pain when an accident happens to you or a loved one?

As grim as it may be, few decisions are more important than planning for your passing. Myriad options exist to help you decide what to do once you or a loved one is gone.

Marriage is a partnership, one that can sour and eventually dissolve. Knowing how to protect your assets and reach a fair settlement will help soften the blow should such a disruptive event happen to you.

True tales of heirs' losses and gains help establish the groundwork needed to maximize the gifts you give or receive during an estate settlement.

THE TEAM

Editorial Directors I John Persinos and Anne Saita
Contributing Editor I Jonathan W. Holasek
Creative Director I Mike Gibson
Production Manager I Rob Hudgins

Group Publisher, Book Division I Eric S. Green
COO I Stan Genkin
CEO I Larry Genkin

FOREWORD

As the Q&A columnist at *Kiplinger's Personal Finance Magazine,* I receive a ton of questions from people in their 20s and 30s who are craving financial advice that can help them get off to a great start. They understand how smart moves now can make a huge difference in their future finances, and they want to know how to make the most of their retirement plan in their first job, save for a first home in a crazy real estate market, stretch their limited starting salary, or get out from under student loan debt.

When I get questions like these, I usually call Brian Jones for advice. Brian has the unique perspective of being both a Certified Financial Planner specializing in young professionals, and also a young professional himself. That's a key reason why he is such an excellent resource. He helps his clients deal with these issues every day and, as a second-generation financial planner, he's known about these valuable strategies for years. Yet he never has the condescending attitude that so many older financial advisors have towards young people. He knows from experience how understanding some key concepts early on can make financial planning so much easier for the rest of your life.

I'm very glad that Brian is finally sharing these essential financial strategies in a book that everyone can learn from. It's a refreshing change from most financial-planning guides that are targeted towards older families with more money, or written by a father-like figure who looks down on the readers. Brian is one of you—a young professional who also happens to have years of experience and can tell you exactly what you need to know to get started. And he makes the concepts interesting by focusing on the real-life stories of real people, who are dealing with the same issues as you are.

I've learned a lot from Brian through the years. I hope that you do, too.

Kimberly Lankford, *Kiplinger's Personal Finance Magazine*

BOOK ACKNOWLEDGEMENTS

The simple fact that this book ever made it to print is a miracle. When I sat down and actually looked at what was involved in the process for someone who had never written a book before, the task at hand seemed almost impossible. There are a number of individuals who played an active role in turning what was once a bunch of random ideas into a reality.

First and foremost I need to thank **Ben Lewis** of **Perception Inc.** I've had the opportunity to know and work with Ben since 2002. Without Ben, this book would not have been possible. His commitment and belief in the project from day one was instrumental in this process. Thanks, Ben.

To **Kim Lankford**. THANK YOU THANK YOU THANK YOU for your help and encouragement while the book was in its infancy. Your ideas and energy were so important at a time when I didn't think the book had a leg to stand on.

To **Debbie Delardi** who taught me *everything* I know about the financial planning industry.

To **Larry Genkin** and **Eric Green** of Larstan Business Reports. Thanks for giving a totally unknown author an opportunity.

To **Dan Vaughan**, **Martha Sotelo**, **Donna Fincher**, **Pat Vaughan** and **Diane Yawn** at **Vaughan, Fincher & Sotelo, PC**. Dan, et al provided some of the key stories in the estate planning chapter as well as oversight and recommendations regarding the estate planning section. Without their help this chapter would not have been possible, so a special "Thanks" to all.

To **Christen Rice** and **Jessica (JD) Smith**. Thanks for all your help on this project.

To **John Persinos, Anne Saita, John Remondini** and **Michael Gibson**. Without all of you, this would never have been completed.

To **John Persil** of **Cocke, Szpanka & Taylor, CPAs, PC**. Thanks for always offering prudent advice and words of encouragement, from the start of this project all the way to completion.

Thanks to all of my colleagues at **Cooper, Jones & McLeland, Ltd.** for their support and encouragement. A very special thanks goes out to **Kim McLeland** for his patience and tolerance with this entire process.

To all my friends, family members, and colleagues who shared stories with me for this book. While some stories made it into the book, a lot of them did not. Your openness and candid comments regarding situations you encountered in your lives will resonate with readers on a level my own words could not. Thank you.

And last but not least, to my mother **Mary Ellen Jones**. She's an incredible woman and mother, and I realize how truly blessed I am to have such a person in my life. Mom was and continues to be one of my biggest fans and sources of encouragement. She's always known when to verbalize her support, and when a simple hug would get her point across. Thanks, mom.

To my wife Amy.

To my father. I've had the greatest of opportunities to work with him, since my very first day in this business. He has instilled in me the conviction, integrity, and pride that guide all that he does in his personal and professional lives. I am a better man because of it.

CHAPTER 1

CASH IS KING

"I NEED MONEY—THAT'S WHAT I WANT." — THE BEATLES

Snap quiz: What's the No. 1 reason for marital discord and split-ups? If you thought "infidelity," think again. The answer is: money woes. The fact is, the biggest problem that every household in America faces is cash—or lack thereof.

Cash is king. Children are taught from a very young age that if they leave a tooth under a pillow the "tooth fairy" will leave them money. This little "lesson" instills in children a very basic and fundamental need: Cash will allow them to purchase something. And thus, thousands upon thousands of new consumers are unleashed into a world full of advertisements that convince them they cannot live without the next greatest rotisserie oven.

Cash makes the world go round. Without it, we'd be forced to write more checks, which just ticks off the people in line behind you at the grocery store.

GETTING STARTED

But with cash flow comes great responsibilities. For many people, these responsibilities sometimes get out of control when they allow themselves to live a lifestyle that is simply beyond what their cash flow will support. This is where things turn ugly and bad things start to happen.

The key to cash flow is to make sure you have cash left over at the end of the month after you've paid all your bills—this is known as "positive" cash flow. The only entity that can legally operate with a "negative" cash flow month in and month out for years on end—and indefinitely spend more money than it takes in on a regular basis—is the United States government. However, if you ran your household like the government, you would end up in jail.

THE SIX KEYS TO POSITIVE CASH FLOW

Positive cash flow can be achieved a number of different ways, but we're going to focus on six of the most important things you and/or your family can do to help you achieve positive cash flow:

1. Not falling prey to "moving on up"
2. Coupons
3. Saying NO to impulse buys
4. Controlling your lifestyle
5. Learning to cook
6. Setting limits on your annual vacation

Let's examine each item in greater detail:

MOVING ON UP

The first step to achieving positive cash flow is to not fall prey to "moving on up" (with apologies to George Jefferson). What is "moving on up"? It's living beyond your means. This is a naturally occurring syndrome that happens to everyone. Yes, everyone. Bill Gates, Donald Trump and

CASH IS KING

> **IN OUR INSTANT GRATIFICATION CONSUMER CULTURE, LIVING BEYOND OUR MEANS HAS BECOME THE AMERICAN WAY. THAT'S WHY CONSUMER DEBT, ESPECIALLY CREDIT CARD DEBT, IS OUT OF CONTROL.**

Shaquille O'Neal all experienced this process, as did your parents and grandparents. In our instant gratification consumer culture, living beyond our means has become the American way. That's why consumer debt, especially credit card debt, is out of control.

You probably never noticed it, but it even happened to you. Moving on up occurs when you graduate from college and start to work for the first time in your life. You are making more money than you have ever made up to this point. This causes a reaction in the back of one's mind to say, "Hey, I've got more money now than I have ever had at any other point in time...let's go spend it!"

Through the process of moving on up, as your income increases, so does your consumption of goods and services. As your salary increases,

INSIDER NOTES The key to cash flow is to make sure you have cash left over at the end of the month after you've paid all your bills—this is known as "positive" cash flow. The only entity that can legally operate with a "negative" cash flow month in and month out for years on end—and indefinitely spend more money than it takes in on a regular basis—is the United States government. However, if you ran your household like the government, you would end up in jail.

you eat better, you eat out more, you buy nicer things and more of them, you take nicer vacations and you get a nicer car.

Fighting this process can be difficult for some, and easy for others. Those who do not feel a very strong emotional attachment to material goods usually have no problems keeping the "moving on up" under control. It is those individuals who are easily swayed by marketers and friends upon whom "moving on up" can have a very powerful grip. The key, to echo Nancy Reagan's anti-drug slogan, is to "Just Say No." Put the credit cards away (we'll cover this in Chapter 2) and leave your wallet at home if you have to go to the mall. Admittedly, that's easier said than done in a society where consumers are subjected to an incessant barrage of commercials exhorting them to buy, buy and buy. But take a deep breath and remember: You shouldn't define your worth as a human being by the material possessions you accumulate and the kind of car your drive. There's no law (not yet, anyway!) that compels you to keep up with the Joneses.

Don't get me wrong. Moving on up has, and does to this day, occur in my household. (When I say "my household," I am including my wife, because if I don't, the floggings are swift and plenty.) However, we try not to eat out more than a few times a month and since we both can't stand to shop, we keep spending on new material goods to a minimum.

COUPONS

The second step to achieving positive cash flow is coupons. Sounds old-fashioned, but they're a time-honored way to maximize your cash flow. Coupons = free money. You just have to go to the effort of clipping the ones for stuff that you use, and remember to use them when you go to the store. Herein lies the problem.

HOME IS WHERE THE IMPULSE LIES

If you want to see impulse buying turned into a science, just amble through the aisles of Home Depot.

What Home Depot has clearly spelled out for consumers, and I think this is brilliant on its part, is that it can calculate, to the square foot, what the sales are per square foot in each store. This allows management the ability to take smaller items and pack them neatly in conspicuous places near the check-out lines and on the ends of aisles. You are literally forced to look at all the new books that show you how to use bricks and mortar to make the barbecue pit you have always longed for.

Home Depot's managers are shrewd indeed, as reflected by the company's healthy bottom line. A May 2004 Home Depot online news release reported record first quarter net earnings of $1.1 billion, or $0.49 per diluted share, up 26 percent for the first quarter of fiscal year 2004, compared with $907 million, or $0.39 per diluted share, for the same time in the previous fiscal year.

In addition, Home Depot reported that it had experienced "the third quarter of sequential improvement in sales per square foot, which increased 3.9 percent to $376.80."

I'm not dumping on Home Depot. In fact, Home Depot is the only store (next to Lowe's) that you can actually get me to shop at on the weekend. Like most adult grown males, I would rather chew off my arm than go to the mall and compete with roving wolf packs of teenagers, just to purchase a new T-shirt.

As a child I remember how exciting it was to go to the local toy store and just drool over the newest and latest creations. Today, I like to keep this tradition alive by visiting Home Depot on the weekends and making a beeline to my favorite "toy" section: the power tools. I don't know what on earth I would need a Flux Core 85 Gasless Wire Feed Welder Kit for, but I do know that I need one in my garage. No home is complete without one!

So, even though I advise you to keep impulse buying to a minimum, I'm not counseling a joyless existence, either.

My mother used to clip coupons (she still does), and as I went off to college and out into the world on my own, I simply got away from this habit. My wife takes the Sunday paper every week and with a pair of scissors clips coupons. I am sure to not get in her way about this. We once came home on a Sunday afternoon after a weekend at the beach and our Sunday paper was missing (coupons too). We made a special trip that afternoon to the grocery store to pick up a paper so we could clip our coupons. The key here is a steady application of discipline.

Look at it this way: coupons lower the monthly grocery bill. Since everyone spends money on groceries several times a month, clipping coupons can work for everyone, no matter your financial situation.

SAYING NO TO IMPULSE BUYS

The third step to positive cash flow is saying NO to all the impulse buys that the sneaky store clerks station near the check-out line. I know what you are thinking, "There is no way the store management and product companies who pay for shelf space at eye level in stores would deliberately go out of their way to load you up with extras before you check out. Inconceivable!" Or is it? The sidebar on Home Depot sheds some light on the issue.

Competition among products for coveted space near the cash register is quite fierce. Remember, between the everyday ad blitz from marketers and the rows and rows of impulse items placed at the check-out line, it is getting harder for consumers to say no to the constant pressure to buy this and buy that. But be strong and say no. Your pocketbook, and ultimately your cash flow, will reflect your strong conviction to limit your closets, bookshelves and drawers to only manageable levels of crap.

CONTROLLING YOUR LIFESTYLE

The fourth step to positive cash flow is controlling your lifestyle. This is a hard pill to swallow sometimes, because the reality of the situation is a very small percentage of people in the world will ever attain the kind of wealth most magazines, newspaper advertisements and television commercials glamorize. The fact that your lifestyle does not match the lifestyle of those presented on MTV's *Cribs* or Robin Leech's *Lifestyles of the Rich and Famous* should not depress you into believing that you are not as well off as your neighbors and/or family, etc.

Lifestyle is really about how you choose to use your money. There are those people who spend every dime they ever make on trendy clothes, flashy cars, cavernous homes and other expensive toys. They never save a dime. The best example I ever saw was a couple who had a really nice lifestyle (two Jaguars, a mansion in the suburbs, expensive clothes and

INSIDER NOTES We Americans love to have someone else cook and prepare our meals for us. Not that there is anything wrong with this. It's nice to be waited on! But if you are serious about achieving (and maintaining) positive cash flow, the cost of restaurant meals should be compared with the cost of buying the food and preparing it yourself.

DINNER OUT AT SWEET WATER TAVERN

Roasted Half Young Chicken with basil redskin mashed potatoes	$12/each
Dinner for two ($24) plus a pint each of Snakebite Black & Tan	$4.07/pint
Cost of dinner out without tax or tip	$32.14
Total cost of dinner with sales tax (4.5%) plus tip (20%) equals	$40.30
Cost of buying a Perdue whole 5lb. Oven Stuffer chicken	$6
Dinner for two ($6) plus pint each of Guinness	($1.33/each)
Cost of 6 redskin potatoes at $1/lb	$1.69
Cost of dinner in for two	$10.35
Total cost savings	$29.95

three vacations a year) and about $150,000 saved between the two of them. And did I forget to mention he is in his late 50s and wants to retire in six years with $300,000 a year in income? Great example for why you should always pay yourself first and save a portion of your paycheck every month—use your 401(k) plan first—from the day you get your first paycheck. No excuses. Save from day one so you can avoid being like this couple.

One of our society's biggest fascinations that compels us to spend millions upon millions of dollars a year is the automobile. They get us from point A to point B regardless of how good they look, require a weekly dose of gasoline (as I write this gas, prices are well over $2/gallon in most of the U.S.), are prone to breaking down (and always at the worst possible time, I might add) and must be replaced continuously throughout your lifetime.

Remember this helpful rule the next time you think you need another vehicle: If your most recent TV appearance was not on *Lifestyles of the*

Rich and Famous, then maybe you should not own more than one car. Period. In addition, the consumption of gasoline on a weekly basis is an ongoing negative cash flow expense that can eat into your bottom line. The case study on page 27 speaks for itself!

LEARN TO COOK

The fifth step to achieving positive cash flow is to learn to cook. What I am really saying is to curb the amount of times you eat out on a monthly basis.

Here's a fact for you: 2004 marked the 13th consecutive year of real sales growth for the restaurant industry. That year the National Restaurant Association forecast industry sales to top $440 billion. On a typical day, the restaurant industry then posted average sales of more than $1.2 billion.

I think these statistics are interesting for two reasons. First, the amount spent on a daily basis to eat out is staggering. Second, there have been five recessions since 1971 (1973-1974, 1980, 1981-1982, 1990-1991, 2001-2002) and yet sales have increased every year, even during those periods of time. We Americans love to have someone else cook and prepare our meals for us. Not that there is anything wrong with this. It's nice to be waited on! But if you are serious about achieving (and maintaining) positive cash flow, the cost of restaurant meals should be compared with the cost of buying the food and preparing it yourself.

The bad news is buying raw food and preparing it yourself is work. Ugh. More work. Just what working people and their families don't need. The good news is that buying the food and preparing it yourself is cheaper and prevents you and/or your family from paying an exponential amount more to have someone else prepare and cook it for you. These cost savings add to the bottom line on a monthly basis (see sidebar, page 22).

GETTING STARTED

Not sure how to cook chicken on the grill? How about preparing a turkey? Or how about making a vegetarian chili that would be ready for you by the time you come home at the end of a busy workday? I have the answer for you and your family: buy a slow cooker.

The slow cooker is the saving grace of my household, keeping both members of my household happy after a long day at work. The slow cooker is really easy, because there is no cooking involved. It does it for you! All you have to do is drop the ingredients in, set it and, when you come home after a long day at work, serve it. Tah-dah! Then you have more family time for important things, like arguing over who is going to clean the slow cooker!

While cooking may not be as trendy or sophisticated as eating at a popular restaurant, the fact that you ate within 15 minutes of walking in the door and now you have the rest of the night to spend by yourself or with your family should leave you feeling like you accomplished what many Americans can't. You saved money by not eating out and you increased your positive cash flow.

SETTING LIMITS ON YOUR ANNUAL VACATION

The last step to achieving positive cash flow is controlling the amount of money you spend on your annual vacation. I can hear you now: "My vacation, too?! You cut back my moving on up; force me to clip coupons; eliminate my fun impulse purchases; downsize my car; tell me to eat out less often...and now you want to take away the last semblance of happiness that I have, my vacation?"

The answer is: Yes. I do. Well, okay, not entirely. The point I am trying to get across is that you do not have to spend one or two percentage points of the U.S. Gross Domestic Product (GDP) just to have fun. Going into debt to fund your vacation is hardly relaxing. If you plan

CASH IS KING

FUN, FUN, FUN ('TILL THEY TAKE THE SUV AWAY)

CASE STUDY

The following is an actual story that happened to a young college graduate many years ago. This case study combines insights into two dilemmas: moving on up and controlling your lifestyle. As you will see, the graduate demonstrated an ability to control and rectify the situation.

As a recent graduate from college, the first thing Bob did was head on out and buy a Ford Expedition with all the bells and whistles. This SUV was enormous and had a 25-gallon gas tank that when filled with gas (87 octane) at $2.12/gallon, cost him about $53. It is safe to assume that he filled the gas tank once a week for the year, costing him $2,756/year.

Two thousand, seven hundred and fifty-six dollars! Think about having to write a check that big. For most of us, that is a good-sized pile of change. If you think $2,756 is not that much, try this exercise. Given the option of pocketing $2,756 or watching two thousand, seven hundred and fifty-six brand new dollar bills sprayed down with lighter fluid and set on fire, which do you choose? If you are a sane and rational person, you would pocket the $2,756. If $2,756 is of little consequence to you, then please put down this book and go do something else.

Eventually Bob got tired of paying $50+ a shot to fill up the tank, so he wisely downsized. He bought a more economical Subaru Outback with a 14-gallon gas tank. To fill the tank with gas (87 octane) at $2.12/gallon costs $29.68. Assuming Bob filled the gas tank once a week for the year, the cost is $1,543/year. This is a cost savings of $1,213 on an annual basis.

Let's get smart here and put this into real dollars. If you invest this difference in filling your gas tank annually for the next 30 years at 7 percent (assuming historical rates of return for large cap stocks at 12% and corporate bonds at 5.5%, in a 65/35 balanced portfolio, and not assuming any income tax obligations, brokerage costs, transaction costs or mutual fund expenses), it gives you an additional $114,547 for retirement. Maybe now you can understand the importance of controlling your lifestyle, especially when it comes to the car you drive.

on taking a vacation, it should be paid for before you leave. If you have to save some of your paycheck on a monthly basis to fund your vacation throughout the year, then do so.

Use this rule of thumb when it comes to funding your vacation: don't spend more than 5% of your gross annual income on your vacation throughout the calendar year. (I call this "The 5% Rule.")

EXAMPLE: For a couple making $100,000 gross annual income with no kids. The 5% Rule means they can spend *up to* $5,000 annually.

Take the same couple, same income and add two little people (herein referred to as children). The 5% Rule means they can spend $5,000 less two kids equals $3,000 annually. That is plenty for a nice week at the beach, the mountains or on the road in the RV.

Note: The 5% rule only works if you a) have no consumer debt (read: credit cards and student loans) and b) your mortgage payments and car payments are manageable (read: an $800/month car payment is not manageable for someone who makes $40,000/year, and I don't care what the salesman who sold you the car said). The 5% Rule also gets a little funny when you have little people or if you are retired, because when you are retired, every day is a vacation.

If you have little people (children, toddlers, babies, rug rats, heathens, etc.) you will need to deduct 1% off your vacation budget for each child. Yes, that's right: a full 1%. Your ability to afford a vacation decreases exponentially with each child you raise. Bummer. The 5% Rule really gets bent out of shape (read: no longer applicable) when you have more than two children. For a number of large families, the 5% Rule simply does not apply because it is not a realistic measure based on the number of mouths in the household.

The 5% Rule is only a suggested guideline. It is not an absolute measure that will apply to all situations and circumstances. But the bottom line remains the same. No matter how much you think you need a ritzy getaway, remember: A vacation should always be paid for before you board that airplane, boat or automobile. Going into debt to pay for a vacation is really no vacation at all.

If you follow these six steps (or at least most of them), then your cash flow is probably well in hand and this book has been a review for you up to this point. If your cash flow is under control and you have more left over at the end of the month after all the bills and savings are done, you are on top of things and have laid an excellent base upon which to enhance your current situation.

If you are not totally in control of your cash flow, do not fret. It is possible to change your particular situation through determination and a little hard work. Many people are in your situation. The difference is that you have made a commitment to fix these shortcomings just by picking up this book.

WHERE DO YOU STAND TODAY?
A WORKSHEET FOR DETERMINING CASH FLOW

These simple calculations will help you take financial inventory by figuring out your cash flow. With a thorough understanding of the financial base that your existing position provides, you can start planning for the future. Then you can determine how to best allocate your resources.

Income	Total for Year	Monthly Average
Take-home salary	$_____	$_____
Dividends, interest, capital gains	$_____	$_____
Job-related bonuses	$_____	$_____
Other income	$_____	$_____
Total income	$_____	$_____

Expenditures		
Savings (401(k), 403(b), etc.)	$_____	$_____
Mortgage/rent	$_____	$_____
Taxes not withheld from salary	$_____	$_____
Food	$_____	$_____
Utilities	$_____	$_____
Insurance premiums	$_____	$_____
Household upkeep	$_____	$_____
Auto (gas, repairs, etc.)	$_____	$_____
Other transportation	$_____	$_____
Recreation	$_____	$_____
Loan payments	$_____	$_____
Credit card interest	$_____	$_____
Non-reimbursable medical bills	$_____	$_____
Clothing	$_____	$_____
Daycare	$_____	$_____
Misc.	$_____	$_____

Add'l after-tax savings	$_____	$_____
Total expenditures:	$_____	$_____
Total income	$_____	$_____
Minus total expenditures	$_____	$_____
Surplus (+) or deficit (-)	$_____	$_____

CASH FLOW TIPS

Here are a few additional hints to help get you on your way towards positive cash flow in your house:

1. Track your expenses. Save your receipts, cash withdrawals from the ATM, etc., and put them into a spreadsheet every week. After two months, examine where you spend your money. Do you remember what you purchased on the $200 Costco visit? How about the $150 trip to Old Navy?

2. Modify accordingly. Are those Starbucks double shot espressos catching up with your checkbook? Is $8/day for lunch at Jerry's Subs & Pizza starting to make you look (and feel) like the Stay Puft Marshmallow Man? Try cutting back on some of these variable expenses. You just have to make a conscientious decision to change the way you spend your money.

3. Pay yourself first. Always pay yourself first by saving money to your emergency fund and retirement fund (we'll cover these in later

INSIDER NOTES No matter how much you think you need a ritzy getaway, remember: A vacation should always be paid for before you board that airplane, boat or automobile. Going into debt to pay for a vacation is really no vacation at all.

chapters). People have asked me if they should stop saving and pay off credit cards or vice versa. My theory is keep saving *and* pay off those debts. My experience has been that if you have debt now, you are more likely to have it in the future, so postponing those savings only puts you further in the hole.

4. Live within your means. If you are making $50,000/year, you do not make enough money to drive a $50,000 automobile. Period. Even if you can *make* the monthly payments, you cannot *afford* the monthly payments. Save your wallet and your money. Put your ego aside, get yourself something more economical and put the savings into your retirement plan and your future.

5. Commit to saving your future pay increases NOW. Sometimes I hear people say that they just can't save a dime at this point. Fine. Then the next time your employer gives you a pay increase, commit to saving 100% of that into your 401(k) plan at work. It is money you never had in the first place and you will not miss it since you are still making your regular salary. Over an 8- to 10-year period and several pay increases, you could be putting 8-10% into your 401(k) plan without modifying your existing lifestyle.

While there are other areas of cash flow that we did not touch on, like funding your qualified retirement plan at work [401(k), 403(b), 457, etc.] and credit cards, we will cover these topics in greater detail in later chapters.

CASH FLOW TO-DO LIST:

1. Develop a cash flow statement (see worksheet, pages 28-29).
2. Modify accordingly and stick to it.

CHAPTER 2

DEBT: SEEING RED

> ## "IF ONE WANTS TO GET OUT AND STAY OUT OF DEBT, HE SHOULD ACT HIS WAGE."
> ## — PROVERB

According to Cardweb.com, in any given month Americans owe $677 billion to bank credit card issuers. The next-closest country: the British, who owe $97 billion per month.

Debt. Can't live with it, can't live without it. The ease of the credit card swipe has long replaced the need to carry cash and stand in line at an ATM for withdrawals. Today the magic of the credit card and its ease of use is everywhere in our society. Need cash? Let your friendly cashier at the grocery store hook you up without a trip to the bank. Need some extra spending money for the weekend? No problem. Credit card issuers have partnered with every major store or restaurant you could visit on a daily basis, like McDonald's (which partnered recently with

American Express), to introduce plastic payment to thousands of restaurants. Plastic is everywhere, and it is here to stay.

But is all this ease of use becoming too much temptation for Americans? Each day Americans charge more and more consumable goods to their credit cards and fall deeper and deeper into debt. Once-manageable payments become too large of a negative monthly expense and the bills mount over time. Late payments, additional charges, harassing phone calls from bill collectors and even the possibility of bankruptcy are not enough of a deterrent to keep average Americans from spending themselves into oblivion. But there is hope.

GOOD DEBT VS. BAD DEBT

The writer David Evans, in the February 23, 2004, issue of *Fortune* magazine, made this interesting point: "In 5,000 years there have been only four times that we have changed the way we pay: There was barter to coinage, coinage to paper, paper to checks, and then checks to credit cards."

As you ponder this paradigm-shift in human society, one thing to remember is that there is "good debt" and "bad debt." Huh? You thought all debt was bad? Not true. A mortgage payment that allows

INSIDER NOTES Credit cards and automobile loans fall into the "bad debt" category. These items are, month in and month out, sapping monthly cash flow and denying you the ability to deploy these resources elsewhere. This "bad debt" is what a majority of Americans struggle with on a daily basis because they have not mastered the notion of following Nancy Reagan's advice: "Just say no."

WHERE THE LIVIN' IS HIGH

CASE STUDY

Back in 1997 I had the opportunity to meet a couple in their middle 40s. Let's call them Mr. and Mrs. Johnson. The Johnsons were a young couple with two daughters, ages 17 and 14. Both Mr. and Mrs. Johnson had jobs outside the home; consequently, they had great cash flow (over $150k on an annual basis back then). They had a mortgage that was within reason and said their primary concern was that their oldest daughter was headed into her senior year of high school but they hadn't saved a dime for college. They were looking for options.

It became very apparent after several minutes that the couple had a spending problem. In hindsight, they had a big spending problem. They had a hard time agreeing on much at the table and that appeared to carry over into their spending habits. After a few minutes the source of their problems was revealed: 15+ credit cards and over $110,000 in credit card debt.

SOME SIMPLE MATH:

An annual interest rate of 16% per year on $110,000 in credit cards equals over $17,000 in interest payments alone. That translates into monthly payments (just interest, no principal payments) of over $1,400/month!

This family was in a big hole and digging deeper and deeper every month. I was always taught that the first step to fixing a problem was identifying the fact that you actually had a problem. She felt they had a problem. He did not think their situation was really a "problem, but more of a short-term inconvenience." The bottom line was they couldn't pay their monthly bills, let alone fund college for their daughters. But that's not the worst part of the situation.

The kids suffer because mom and dad can't seem to control their spending habits. Now their children will be at a significant disadvantage if they can't afford to pay the bills for college.

While some helpful hints on managing the existing problem were recommended to Mr. and Mrs. Johnson, the simple fact was they could not agree on their "problem." This lack of agreement was a sign that this "situation" would continue for some time into the future. Unfortunately, I do not know what happened to Mr. and Mrs. Johnson and whether or not they were ever able to pay off the credit card debt and send their daughters to college.

The situation with Mr. and Mrs. Johnson highlights a very important fact about our society today. You have two things you can do with your money after you get your paycheck; you can spend it or you can save it. We all have to spend it to an extent (mortgage payment, food, satellite radio, iPod downloads, etc.), but there comes a point in time, or at least there should, when enough is enough. This couple could not say "enough" and it showed. Now their marriage and their family were starting to strain under the weight of the obligations they had created.

you to afford the "American Dream" (more on this in Chapter 5) is good debt. You are not only purchasing a major asset over time through the use of leverage, but you also get a pretty good tax break for doing so.

Picture this: It's a bright sunny day and you stroll out to your mailbox to see what goodies the postman has left for you. You open the mailbox, reach inside and pull out an overflowing handful of magazines, credit card offers, catalogs and a credit card bill. You think to yourself, "Well, it shouldn't be that high this month, I only ate out a

> **DEBT IS NOT MANAGEABLE WHEN THE MONTHLY PAYMENTS DETRACT FROM YOUR ABILITY TO RUN THE HOUSEHOLD, PAY FOR GROCERIES, LIVING EXPENSES AND SAVE.**

few times and filled my car with a couple of tanks of gas." But when you get inside and open up the credit card bill, you see that you charged a little bit more than you remember. In fact, your credit card balance is so large that you need two pages just to cover all the activity from the previous month.

Credit cards and automobile loans fall into the "bad debt" category. These items are, month in and month out, sapping monthly cash flow and denying you the ability to deploy these resources elsewhere. This "bad debt" is what a majority of Americans struggle with on a daily basis because they have not mastered the notion of following Nancy Reagan's advice: "Just say no."

My parents taught me that debt is purely a function of cash flow. If you have the cash flow to pay for the purchase all up front (not a novel idea but rarely practiced anymore) or the ability to meet monthly payment obligations like a mortgage, then the debt is manageable. Debt is not manageable when the monthly payments detract from your ability to run the household, pay for groceries and other living expenses and save.

If you want a lower-stress household, you need to keep debt payments to a level where the payments don't negatively affect your activities, how you spend your free time or consume a majority (read: more than 50%) of the total income that comes into the household on a monthly basis. If your debt level is at 50% or higher, then you need to take

some steps to curb your spending habits in order to prevent falling into the situation described in this chapter's case study of financial woe.

JUST ONE WORD: PLASTIC

One of the largest "bad debt" problems facing Americans today is the credit card. According to *CNN/Money*, the national average credit card bill is $9,340. Compare that to the average credit card balance of $3,000 in 1990. Paying $200/month at 16.44% interest rate would take you 6.33 years to pay the card off completely. Providing you don't add to it, of course.

The problem here is that you are diverting $200/month to a credit card when these dollars could be diverted elsewhere to help pay for a monthly mortgage payment, fund college for your children, or contribute to your qualified retirement plan at the office. It may not sound like a lot of money, but $200/month paid out on a monthly basis over a 30-year period of time (assuming a 7% growth rate and no taxes paid on the amount annually or at the end of 30 years) grows to in excess of $243,900!

That said, Americans are not to blame (entirely) for their inability to say no to the credit card's proliferation into every store they could possibly visit. Credit card companies share a portion of the blame. Credit card companies know how profitable credit cards are (this is a $30-billion—yup, billion—dollar-a-year industry) and their shareholders love them for it.

Note: In my household we charge everything on a monthly basis to the credit cards. We use mileage cards to maximize our return on our monthly spending. While this requires extra discipline and due diligence on our part (airline mileage cards typically will charge a higher rate of interest than other credit cards), we make sure we pay the balance off every month. So while a majority of credit card debt/usage can be "bad," if you manage it in a prudent manner it is a very effective way to leverage your expenses on a monthly basis.

AUTOMOBILE LOANS

Let's talk about the single most cumbersome debt that is weighing on individuals and families: automobile loans. Automobile loans are consuming more and more of Americans'

disposable monthly income. As TV shows highlight high-end cars for high-end lifestyles, Americans are digging themselves into financial oblivion trying to live the good life. According to Edmunds.com, the average consumer spends 11% of his or her monthly gross income on a car payment. Yet most Americans aren't even saving that amount into their qualified retirement plans! The words of Albert Einstein come to mind: "Only two things are infinite, the universe and human stupidity, and I'm not sure about the former."

The August 2005 edition of *Worth* magazine reported: "...15% of affluent consumers purchased a luxury automobile last year, according to Unity Marketing's Luxury Report 2005, spending an average of

INSIDER NOTES Automobile loans are consuming more and more of Americans' disposable monthly income. As TV shows highlight high-end cars for high-end lifestyles, Americans are digging themselves into financial oblivion trying to live the good life. According to Edmunds.com, the average consumer spends 11% of his or her monthly gross income on a car payment. Yet most Americans aren't even saving that amount into their qualified retirement plans!

$46,394. This represents a 31% increase over the average cost in 2003." What is fascinating to me is that I see a lot of cars on the road that cost much more than $46,394 and are considered "luxury." So the question becomes: How are we able to afford such high-priced vehicles?

There seems to be a misconception in our society that if you are making $100,000/year, you can afford to purchase a 2005 BMW 750Li, complete with a 4.8-liter Valvetronic V8 engine that produces 360 hp and goes from 0 to 60 in just 5.8 second and includes thirteen 420-watt speakers and six-disc CD changer. All for a mere $74,500!

*Disclaimer: This is not a new car advertisement. I love nice cars just as much as the next person, especially this model sedan from BMW. I hope to have one myself one day when I can really afford it (read: When I can pay cash for it).

You can't afford this vehicle (unless you pay cash entirely for this purchase) if you're making $50,000/year. You can't afford this vehicle if you make $100,000/year. I'm willing to bet that you probably can't afford this car even if you make $150,000/year. I'm assuming that if you make $150k on an annual basis, then you at least own your own home and pay a mortgage of at least $3,000/month and save the

INSIDER NOTES If you buy a mammoth-sized SUV that only gets 12 mpg in the city, you will make more trips to the pump than your neighbor in a hybrid. That is not a slam on owning an SUV; it is just a fact. You will spend more of your positive cash flow every week, month and year on gas than your neighbor. If you can't afford the gas—i.e., if you complain about the price at the pump—you can't afford the vehicle.

THE HIGH PRICE OF STATUS

Let's take the 2005 BMW 750Li, starting at $74,500. Suppose our buyer has some cash to put down, say 20%.

	$74,500
Less Downpayment	($14,900)
Total amount to finance	
(less taxes, tags, freight, all the usual BS the dealers throw in)	$59,600
Assuming a finance charge of 3.5% for four years, your monthly payment would be	$1,332.42

Seems high, doesn't it? Ah, but the automobile manufacturers have another trick up their sleeve! It's called "Why finance the car of your dreams for four years when you can finance it for six (or seven) years and REALLY lower your monthly payment!" Bad idea. It is an even worse idea than buying the car in the first place.

The monthly payment for a six-year loan will not be at the same 3.5% rate as the four-year loan. There is more "risk" for the automobile manufacturer, so to compensate for this risk they will increase the loan interest rate. For purposes of our example, let's increase the interest rate to 5.5% for six years. If we do this, the monthly payment declines to $973.74. While this does lower your monthly payment, the total price of the car increased since you lengthened the time period of your loan.

Four years of $1,332.42/month equals total payments of $63,956.16. Six years of $973.74/month equals total payments of $70,109.28.

The total cost of financing the BMW six years over the original purchase price increases the cost of the vehicle by $10,509.28 or in

percentage terms by approximately 17.63%. This is why automobile manufacturers can offer extras like "dealer cash back" and such reduced prices on cars. They make up the profit on the finance charges because most Americans are too "busy" to notice they are paying more over time for their vehicles.

Wait, it gets better. Financing a car over a longer period of time has another unseen "benefit" that most people fail to think about until they have had a car accident. You see, insurance companies don't really care how long you finance your car or how big your car loan. The insurance companies will only pay you for what your car is worth, say, if your car is totaled in an automobile accident.

So, let's say you purchase your $74,500 BMW 2005 750Li and a year later, when you still owe $54,000 (estimated loan value) on the car, it is totaled in a car accident that is your fault. The good news is that you have insurance. The bad news is that the insurance company will cut you only a check for $45,000. The really bad news is you owe more than that on your loan.

This is called being "upside down" on your loan. You owe more than the car is worth. The insurance company "will pay the agreed upon actual cash value of your property subject to the terms and conditions of your policy" (from a leading insurer's website) and since your loan amount is higher than the value, you get to make up the difference. You can't see it, but you can sure feel it, if and when the time comes.

Another invisible commitment with automobiles is gasoline. Per gallon prices of $2.00, $3.00 or even $4.00 may be the expected norms for years to come. There are lots of reasons for the high price of gasoline at the pump, but as busy Americans we typically only focus on what it costs us every time we head to the pump.

If you buy a mammoth-sized SUV that only gets 12 mpg in the city, you will make more trips to the pump than your neighbor in a hybrid. That is not a slam on owning an SUV; it is just a fact. You will spend more of your positive cash flow every week, month and year on gas than your neighbor. If you can't afford the gas— i.e., if you complain about the price at the pump—you can't afford the vehicle.

The planet is entering an era of increased oil demand from competing nations. The price of gasoline is unlikely to reach bargain levels any time in the near term. To reduce your energy consumption may require prudent and forward thinking on your part when you are considering a new and/or used vehicle for purchase. Every time you go to the pump, money is extracted from your wallet. This money could be leveraged for purposes more useful than propelling several tons of steel down a stretch of asphalt.

maximum into your 401(k) plan at the office on an annual basis. As the religious scholar Esther de Waal put it: "Wealth consists not in having great possessions but in having few wants."

Financing is the automobile manufacturer's gravy train that allows all of us to afford the astronomically priced monstrosities they produce these days. Financing a car is the surest possible way to consume a large portion of your cash flow on a monthly basis and divert these dollars into an investment that never makes money and only depreciates in value over time.

The automobile industry is smart—too smart, actually. They've been plying their trade for more than 100 years, so they know a trick or four. They realize that if they can get consumers to purchase their vehicles and pay for them over time, they can make larger and more expensive vehicles for our consumption. Planned obsolescence keeps us coming back for new models. We Americans love cars and suffer from "road envy." Road envy is the simple principle that we can't stand seeing our next-door neighbor drive a nicer car than we do. Consequently, we buy bigger and more expensive vehicles, and pay for them over time.

CONTROLLING DEBT, BEFORE IT CONTROLS YOU

The bad news is, you may not be able to eliminate debt. At the very least, it is hard to do. Moreover, it may not be the smartest financial decision in the world—after all, a modest amount of leverage does serve a useful purpose. The good news is, there are ways to cut down on the level of debt(s) in your house.

For starters, a smart thing to do on an annual basis is to request a credit report. It helps to know who is checking your credit and to see if your identity has been stolen and frivolous purchases made on your behalf. Better to know sooner rather than later.

HERE'S A LIST OF THE THREE MAJOR CREDIT-REPORTING AGENCIES:
Equifax
P.O. Box 740241
Atlanta, GA 30374
800-685-1111
www.equifax.com

Experian
P.O. Box 2104
Allen, TX 75013
888-397-3742
www.experian.com

Trans Union LLC
Consumer Disclosure Center
P.O. Box 1000
Chester, PA 19022
800-888-4213
www.transunion.com

A credit report can be obtained for a small fee from each agency. By law, credit agencies must send you a complimentary report if you have been denied credit within the past 60 days.

You can also request free credit reports from the website www.annualcreditreport.com or by calling 877-322-8228, where you can make a separate request of each of the three main credit reporting agencies (Equifax, Experian and Trans Union). You can ask for one free credit report from one agency every fourth months; thus, you can now check all three agencies throughout the year for FREE. The price is right!

One of the easier ways to manage the number of credit cards you have is to keep your cards to one or two. There is absolutely no reason you need 10 cards. Avoid store credit cards. The offer of "an additional 10% off today's purchase if you sign up today" is probably not enough of a benefit to you over time to justify taking out another card and opening up another credit line. This extra card is just an incentive to buy more useless stuff to fill up your closets at home.

GETTING STARTED

Admittedly, it is so hard to "just say no" to the Home Depot card, or the Macy's card, or even your beloved college alma mater that now offers a credit card. However, the interest rates on store cards are typically onerous and, besides, you don't need a dozen, or even a half dozen, credit cards. One or two should be more than plenty. Close out old credit cards once you have paid them off and don't accept any of the offers that show up in the mail. You'll thank yourself for simplifying your life and lightening up your wallet or purse.

Another helpful measure to limit the amount of consumer debt in the household is to maintain an emergency fund of at least three to six months' worth of household monthly expenses in cash at all times. This emergency fund is not a slush fund for buying a new pair of Jimmy Choo pumps. This cash account is for EMERGENCIES only.

The following is a list of *acceptable* emergency fund expenditures:
- Heat pump breaks (in the middle of winter, of course) and needs replacing
- Car needs new tires to pass inspection
- Pipe bursts and the plumber has to come out and fix it
- A trip to the emergency room for stitches
- New reading glasses to replace the ones you left on the counter at Starbucks

The following is a list of *unacceptable* emergency fund expenditures:
- A four-night stay in Honolulu
- One wild weekend trip to Las Vegas
- A brand new Trek Madone 5.2 (so you too can be like Lance Armstrong)
- A new Big Bertha Titanium 454 driver
- A 65-inch, DPL, flat plasma screen TV

REAL PEOPLE, REAL LIFE

*I love stories. As a kid, I always found that I
better understood the point my parents were trying to make when
they told me a story instead of lecturing me for hours. The following
two stories are not testimonials; they are real-life stories about actual
people. As with all of the stories in this book, each bestows a valuable
lesson worth emulating.*

» **Laura** is a divorced mother of two children. Her oldest daughter is
grown and independent, while her son is still in high school.
Laura was laid off in early 2000 when the Dot.com Boom became
the Dot.com Bomb. While Laura did have a small severance from
her previous employer, she found it increasingly difficult to find a
job. Interview after interview and months later, Laura had
exhausted her severance payments, exhausted her emergency fund
and was beginning to accumulate credit card debt, which she had
used to fund the day-to-day expenditures in her household.

As Laura borrowed more and more against her credit cards, she
became aware that her financial situation was becoming increasingly tenuous. Laura decided that based on a low interest rate
environment, coupled with the increased appreciation she had in
her primary residence, she would refinance her existing mortgage.
Laura was able to consolidate her credit card debt by rolling the
debt underneath the house (so to speak). Plus, with the lower
interest payment on her mortgage, Laura was able to take out
additional cash to tide her over while she got started at her new
job, and she was able to lower her monthly expenses by
$500/month.

Improving Laura's monthly cash flow (lower mortgage payment plus a monthly paycheck from her new employer) made her household function more smoothly, and she felt more comfortable in general. Laura restored her emergency fund over time and continues to be credit card debt-free.

» **Alice and Tom** are married and in their early 50s. They have two sons in high school, and both Alice and Tom own their own business. Tom runs a home inspection business and Alice runs a management training/consulting business. Both businesses experienced a slowdown in 2000 that lasted roughly 18 months. While Alice had always been meticulous about maintaining cash reserves in both companies as well as in the home, the business slowdown impacted both businesses; eventually, the household was starting to feel the cash crunch.

While business was slowly starting to rebound, Alice and Tom were faced with credit card and business liabilities that were growing in size. Alice and Tom made the decision to liquidate stock that Alice held in a brokerage account. Alice obtained the stock while working for her previous employer, a Fortune 100 company. Since Alice had held the stock for many years, the sale of stock qualified for long-term capital gains tax treatment, or a federal tax rate of 15%, plus she paid an additional 5.75% on the state taxes.

Alice and Tom used the proceeds from the stock sale to reduce their accumulated debts and to give a quick infusion of cash into the household. Eventually both businesses regained their footing and the cash flow situation in their household returned to normal. Alice and Tom's first priority was to replenish the cash reserves in the house and then the businesses.

Where's the best spot to keep your emergency fund? Here are some popular options:

» Checking account (may not earn much interest, but it is liquid)

» Savings account (will earn something, which is always better than nothing)

» Money Market account (typically pays higher rates of interest; please note that a bank money market account may be FDIC-insured whereas a mutual fund money market is not)

» Certificates of Deposit (can be illiquid if you have, say, a one-year CD and you need to break it after three months; consider "laddering" your portfolio with staggered maturities)

The last step to help control your debt is to have the credit card companies remove your name from pre-approved listings. You may request that the consumer credit agencies exclude your name from pre-approved lists by taking action today to decrease the amount of junk mail you receive in the future. To find out more about how to do this, pick up the phone and call 1-888-5OPTOUT (1-888-567-8688). Opting out will limit the number of pre-approved credit card offers, unsolicited credit and insurance offers you receive daily via snail mail. This is a great way to prevent you from being tempted by credit card companies. It also cuts down on all the paper you get in the mail, thereby decreasing the unnecessary decimation of trees.

DEBT TO-DO LIST:

1. Balance Sheet exercise (see www.gettingstartedfinance.com)

2. Cash flow exercise (see worksheet, pages 28-29)

CHAPTER 3

SAYING "I DO"

"MARRIAGE IS THE TRIUMPH OF IMAGINATION OVER INTELLIGENCE."
— DR. SAMUEL JOHNSON

There are unforgettable milestones in everyone's life. Your first day at kindergarten, the first time you ride a bike without training wheels, going off to summer camp, scoring your first soccer goal, your first piano recital, high school graduation, your first day of work after college, your wedding day and so on. The day I asked my wife to marry me was one of the most special days of my life, but I won't bore you with details. I also remember the day *after* I asked her to marry me. It marked the start of what became known in our house as "the wedding planning." At this point, most women smile—while most men run and hide.

The day after I proposed to my wife, she promptly went to the local bookstore and bought every wedding magazine she could find. She

came home with bags of wedding magazines, which I helped her haul through the front door. I asked for her hand in marriage, gave her a very expensive piece of compressed coal set in platinum and in return I got to haul 60 lbs. of wedding magazines into the dining room. But I was not about to ruin her day.

One of the most important issues to rear its head during the initial phase of the wedding planning process is (surprise!) money. Because you are on the verge of throwing quite possibly the most elaborate party of your lives, you want to make sure that there are no snags to spoil the event. So, first things first: You must determine how much to spend on your wedding without going broke.

Your betrothed (or your future mother-in-law) may argue with you on this point, but my firm conviction is that you should not have to mortgage your house or take out a home equity line of credit to pay for a wedding. Since most of us can't convince television executives to turn our wedding day into a two-hour "must-see TV" event, we have to make due with what we have. Set your maximum spending threshold, and then stick to it!

There are two ways to look at wedding funding: Either you are the engaged couple who will spend/save/borrow to make your wedding

INSIDER NOTES One of the most important issues to rear its head during the initial phase of the wedding planning process is (surprise!) money. Because you are on the verge of throwing quite possibly the most elaborate party of your lives, you want to make sure that there are no snags to spoil the event. So, first things first: You must determine how much to spend on your wedding, without going broke.

> ## FOR A LOT OF PEOPLE, THE BEST PART ABOUT PLANNING A WEDDING IS THE REGISTRY.

dreams a reality; or you are prudent parent(s) who are determined to not mortgage your own home to pay for a child's wedding.

My wife and I were given a certain dollar contribution by her parents as well as mine. She and I picked up a few additional expenses on our own. We have had friends who were given more than we were, and some who were given less. We all made do with what we had.

Our wedding was not elaborate compared to what's often showcased in magazines and TV specials. My wife did not wear a $70,000 wedding dress, nor did she arrive with 15 wedding attendants, each in their own separate limousine. We did not have ice sculptures, fireworks or a marching band at our reception. We did not spend $1 million on flowers, as did Brad Pitt and Jennifer Aniston for their Malibu wedding (and look how that marriage turned out). Nor did we leave the reception in a helicopter on our way to the private jet waiting to whisk us off to a secluded beach in Bora Bora. It was a small affair with family and friends who mattered most to us.

Now, for those who are parents (or soon-to-be parents) with the forethought to say, "I do not want to go broke funding my child's wedding," there is a step you can take now to head off financial chaos in the future. Fund a "wedding account" the same way you would fund your own 401(k) plan or your child's college education fund. Start today by saving monthly. That way, when the time comes, you already have accumulated a pile of money for the wedding.

For a lot of people, the best part about planning a wedding is the registry. The wedding registry is akin to a child's Christmas "wish list," only for adults. You enjoy the opportunity to select all the household items that you didn't get around to purchasing prior to getting engaged. You just have to get married, throw a reception and, in return, all your families and friends purchase items on your registry. What a deal! If nothing else, it's a wonderful boost to your cash flow.

I've inserted a few paragraphs here about the wedding registry because it's one of the best parts of the actual wedding planning process. It's not as fun as tasting wedding cake or main course selections, yet it's not as boring as visits to the florist or searching for wedding invitations on-line. The wedding registry allows both the bride and groom to pick out "a few" (ahem) items to help get them started in their new life together.

A wide range of stores offer wedding registries, including Home Depot, Target, Macy's, Crate & Barrel, Pottery Barn and Tiffany's, to name just a few. The hardest part is making your lists ahead of time and actually going to the store to select your items. I highly recommend an actual trip to the mall (note: this coming from the man who would rather chew off his arm than go shopping). And not because of the

INSIDER NOTES Now, for those who are parents (or soon-to-be parents) with the forethought to say, "I do not want to go broke funding my child's wedding," there is a step you can take now to head off financial chaos in the future. Fund a "wedding account" the same way you would fund your own 401(k) plan or your child's college education fund. Start today by saving monthly. That way, when the time comes, you already have accumulated a pile of money for the wedding.

joys of finding a parking space and navigating through sullen, glassy-eyed teenagers who are glued to cell phones. No, I recommend an actual trip to the mall because of a wonderful device known as the wedding registry gift scanner.

The scanner is a handheld device that resembles a water gun. Just point it at the price tag on the item you wish to add to your wedding registry and a really cool red laser beam shines on the tag and records the item. Need four margarita glasses? No problem, just fire the "laser" four times. You can even attempt to "laser" your significant other's butt as you cruise in and out of the aisles. Note to all the men reading this: I found that my continued attempts to "laser" my wife's butt resulted in 1) a dead battery and 2) an unhappy fiancée who felt I wasn't being "serious" enough.

YOURS, MINE AND OURS

In all seriousness, marital finances can be a tricky issue for a lot of people. Some people are more comfortable than others discussing their finances, income, debt, etc. For some the subject of money is a very personal and private matter. Engaged couples must remember that coming together as a single entity requires open and full disclosure of all financially related details by both parties. One party's hiding of financial facts can be extremely detrimental to the new marriage. Before you walk down the aisle, start off on the right foot by reviewing your situations together in detail.

Now might also be a good time to mention that in some cases, a prenuptial agreement may be something worth discussing as well. Unfortunately, marriage is like a business and businesses must be protected in the event the union does not work. This does not mean

that you are planning on the marriage not making it from day one; it just means that you have covered all of the bases and are managing the situation effectively from the start. While this topic can be extremely difficult to broach with your bethrothed, if presented in a non-threatening and positive manner, it is possible that both parties can reach an understanding without beating the other with bats. Make a note to yourself: to surprise your fiancé after your rehearsal dinner with said papers is probably *not* the most opportune moment to have this discussion. Plan accordingly.

If one party brings debts to the table (in the form of, say, student loans, credit card bills, automobile payments or mortgage arrears), and the other party does not, this can be a situation where one party says: "Hey, this is your mess, not mine." But it doesn't work like that in a marriage. Marriage is a two-way street. What's mine is yours, what's yours is mine. Remember your vow? For richer or poorer, baby.

That doesn't necessarily mean that the party without any debt needs to add his or her name to the other party's debt. But what it does mean is now it's both of your debt to pay off together. This can be hard for a lot of couples. It can take time (and negotiation) for someone to accept the fact that marriage is a partnership, and he or she is no longer operating

INSIDER NOTES Engaged couples must remember that coming together as a single entity requires open and full disclosure of all financially related details by both parties. One party's hiding of financial facts can be extremely detrimental to the new marriage. Before you walk down the aisle, start off on the right foot by reviewing your situations together in detail.

SAYING "I DO"

FROM SINGLE OPERATORS TO BUSINESS PARTNERS

CASE STUDY

» **Nancy and Chris** got married in October 2002. They live in Virginia and were married in Washington, D.C. Both work full time for consulting firms and expect to start a family sometime in the next couple of years.

I met Nancy and Chris just about a year prior to their wedding. As with a lot of imminent newlyweds, they had concerns about debt, car payments, mortgage payments and their retirement savings. Nancy and Chris realized that they were not saving as much as they should and opted to make the necessary changes. Just as they modified their wedding expenses to meet their budget, they cut back on their personal spending to accommodate their need to save more. Gadgets, vacations, flashy clothing, fancy new cars, restaurant meals—all of the indulgences that seemed appropriate when they were single were now drastically curtailed, if not eliminated altogether. Cash flow was redirected to long-term goals: a single-family house; college savings for future kids; life insurance; retirement.

Nancy and Chris's wedding went off without a hitch. They both continue to work full time. But as young newlyweds, they continue to grapple with student debt and car payments, in addition to paying the mortgage on a monthly basis. They want a family in the near future, and seem well on their way to achieving this now that they have gotten their finances under control. They've consolidated all of their banking into one joint account and conduct monthly "financial meetings" at the kitchen table. When it comes to money, they practice full disclosure and open communication. They no longer spend money as separate entities; they behave as a business partnership.

as a sole individual. Patience is the key to understanding, and understanding is one of the most important aspects of a good working marriage.

Combining finances is a natural progression for all couples. For two separate households to come together as a single entity all at once is a tough feat to pull off. The newlyweds must consolidate separate automobile and homeowner's insurance policies; separate cell phone carriers; separate residences; separate pots and pans; etc. Does she hate your beloved coffee table that's fashioned from a lobster trap? Do you hate her collection of ceramic dolls? What stays? What goes?

Just getting through the wedding planning and the ceremony is arduous enough. Now, on top of that, throw in the fact that once you're married, everything must be joined together into a single cohesive entity. Your savings, checking and various types of insurance must be integrated. This, my friends, is where the financial rubber hits the marital road.

From my own experience, as well as what I've witnessed of other couples, the merging of two separate households usually takes time and can't be accomplished all at once. Couples tend to start small by first deciding the location of the marital home. What usually follows is

INSIDER NOTES Just getting through the wedding planning and the ceremony is arduous enough. Now, on top of that, throw in the fact that once you're married, everything must be joined together into a single cohesive entity. Your savings, checking and various types of insurance must be integrated. This, my friends, is where the financial rubber hits the marital road.

> **WHAT IF YOUR FIANCÉE IS A "SUPER TYPE A" MEGA-CONTROL FREAK? BE FLEXIBLE AND REMEMBER THAT EVERYONE NEEDS SPACE.**

the merging of all personal assets (pots, pans, TVs, stereos, appliances, furniture, etc.); insurance coverage (some insurance rates drop when you get married); bank accounts; and so on. You can't do it all overnight. Ease into it.

What if your fiancée is a "Super Type A" mega-control freak? Be flexible and remember that everyone needs space. This is especially true when it comes to the finances. If necessary for your future spouse's comfort level, keep separate checking and savings accounts and just create a new joint checking account as a supplement. Deposit all paychecks into the joint account and pay all bills from it. Over time, you will both become comfortable with the idea of a joint account and eventually consolidate all accounts.

Credit cards, mortgages, car loans and investments can all be changed into a jointly held asset (or liability), but only after careful consideration of the time, effort involved and perceived benefits. So one car is in your name and another car is in your spouse's name. Big deal. Don't sweat the small stuff. Finances take time to get worked out and there is no need to race to get all the paperwork and consolidation completed within six months of your wedding. Just keep your eye on the eventual goal of financial consolidation and it will happen incrementally over the months and years.

GETTING STARTED

UNTIL DEATH DO YOU PART

One of the most important financial responsibilities to handle after you're married is to update the beneficiary designations on your life insurance, IRAs, Roth IRAs and any retirement plans you have at your employer(s). Now that you are married, you want to provide for your spouse in the event of your death. One of the easiest and most cost-effective ways of doing this regarding your retirement plans and your life insurance is to designate your spouse as your primary beneficiary.

Making your new spouse your primary beneficiary requires you to fill out a beneficiary change form and sign it. It should take you all of about 60 seconds to complete the form. The form says that at your death, your spouse is entitled to 100% of the account/proceeds, providing they can supply the appropriate documentation, typically a certified death certificate. This type of a beneficiary designation avoids the probate process entirely and does not require the use of an estate planning attorney (more on this in the estate planning section).

Last, but not least, in all the parties and get-togethers that will be held to celebrate impending nuptials, you should always listen to the advice of those who have been married for long periods of time—i.e., 30+ years. My parents told my wife and I to always have realistic expectations of one another and our marriage. A friend sardonically revealed the secret to his happy marriage: "Low expectations." More to the point, we knew our wedding would not be a made-for-TV event with a $4 million budget, so we had to pay attention to costs. We kept it small and simple, and it made us very happy.

Another couple told us to never, ever sweat the small stuff. They told us that no one would ever remember if we served prime rib and crab cakes or chicken and crab cakes. It didn't matter. What mattered was how my wife and I respected and appreciated each other.

At our wedding, we had our picture matted on a frame on which everyone could sign their names and add a line or two of congratulations. My buddy Dave wrote the following aphorism. My wife and I think it is some of the best advice that can be given to a new couple as they head down the road of a long and, hopefully, happy marriage:

"When you're wrong, admit it; when you're right, shut up."

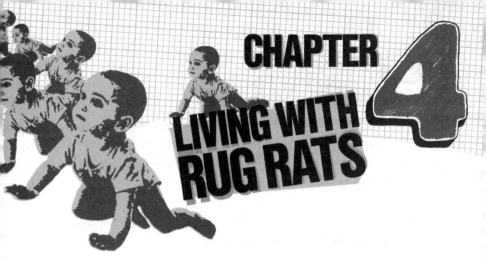

"ENJOY THE LITTLE THINGS IN LIFE, FOR ONE DAY YOU MAY LOOK BACK AND REALIZE THEY WERE THE BIG THINGS."
— HENRY DAVID THOREAU

The decision to start a family by having or adopting children is a major milestone in any person or couple's life. Ask anyone who has raised children and they will tell you that your life as you knew it, prior to children, ceases. Batten down the hatches, because kids are like hurricanes: able to tear into multiple things at the same time; switch direction instantaneously; and run at speeds in excess of 100 mph until they finally lose energy and peter out—only to eventually strike again.

The cost of funding your child/children's college education is second only to funding your own retirement. According to many financial websites, a child born today who attends an out-of-state public college is estimated to incur costs of almost $300,000! On top of this, children

are a negative cash flow expense seven days a week, every month, 12 months a year, for at least 18 years, if not longer. Simply put, kids are very expensive. Are you really ready?

The following anecdote is instructive. My 4-year-old nephew Tyler once spouted the following to his grammy:

TYLER: Gimme some juice.

GRANDMA: What's the magic word, Tyler?

TYLER: Gimme some juice NOW!

(Note: Tyler actually did live long enough to see his fifth birthday.)

Kids say the darnedest things. And they cost a lot of money, too. But ask any parent who has been there and they will tell you that raising a child is without a doubt the most challenging and rewarding experience life has to offer. But this chapter isn't about how to raise your child to grow up and not be a serial killer. There are plenty of other books at the local library that tell you everything you need to know about childrearing. This book is about money.

INSIDER NOTES Most new parents often neglect to update their estate plan because they have been too busy with interrupted sleep schedules, 3 a.m. trips to the pediatrician and changing diapers to pay attention to the idea of updating estate documents, such as the will. This is one of those mistakes that can impact your family for generations. If there are no named guardian(s) for your children, they are considered to be a ward of the state and the state will decide who is best suited to raise your child.

LIVING WITH RUG RATS

THE WAGES OF EXTRAVAGANCE

CASE STUDY

To be instructive, not all stories in this book center on success stories. You can glean important lessons from failures and mistakes. Here's a real-life story of what I consider to be one of the worst ways to pay for your kids' college. I share this only as an example of what not to do.

I met Sally and Bob (not their real names) back in 1998. They both had mid- to senior-level management jobs and their cash flow was what I would consider to be "above average." Sally and Bob had two daughters, ages 17 and 14. Sally and Bob also had a mountain of credit card debt, but that is not the issue in this situation. The problem was their oldest daughter was starting her senior year in high school, and Sally and Bob had not saved a dime for either of their daughters' college expenses. They had spent their daughters' college education funds on their extravagant lifestyle—fancy cars, nice clothes, jewelry, etc.—and now they had absolutely nothing to show for it.

What's more, the local real estate market was moribund, so they didn't have the option of tapping home equity to pay for college. My meeting with them was painful. Sally and Bob had done a terrible job of planning for the future, and their punishment was that their girls would have to obtain massive amounts of student loans in order to pay their tuition bills. Because of the parents' high living, the kids would be saddled with significant college debt for years to come.

Don't let this happen to you and your family. Start saving today for college.

GETTING STARTED

REAL PEOPLE, REAL KIDS

CASE STUDY

» **Brenda and Roger** are married with two children, ages 5 and 2. After several years of marriage, they decided to start a family through adoption. Both of their children were adopted overseas.

Before they adopted their second child, Brenda and Roger wanted to structure their household so that Brenda could remain at home for at least the first few years. Since Brenda was the primary income-earner in the household, this required structuring their investments and cash flow in such a manner as to give them maximum flexibility while at the same time allowing them to continue to run their household while Brenda took time off from the office.

Brenda and Roger decided that repositioning their existing assets to supplement the household cash flow would be enough to replace most of Brenda's income and allow them to continue to operate their household. Certain sacrifices were made: They delayed purchase of a new car; ate out less often; and resisted the urge to buy that new flat-screen HDTV. But through their exertion of financial discipline, Brenda and Roger were able to make their dream a reality by adopting their second child and letting Brenda staying at home for the first year or so.

Brenda told me afterwards: "We have everything we want now and are so happy. The kids are a lot of work sometimes, but it takes just a little smile from them and their saying 'I love you' to make it all worthwhile."

» **Kim and Gene** are married with three children (ages 6, 4 and 2). Kim and Gene started a family right after they married. From the very first day that they brought their first child home from the hospital, they started saving on a monthly basis to pre-fund anticipated college education costs.

After researching the many available options for pre-funding their children's college-related expenses, Kim and Gene decided that a Section 529 college savings plan was the right choice for their particular financial and tax situation. Using an automatic withdrawal from their checking account, each month they set aside a certain dollar amount into a 529 college education savings plan set up for each of the children. (Read more on 529 Plans later in this chapter.)

According to Gene, the idea of borrowing to pay for college is simply not an option. "We want all of the kids' future college education expenses paid for by the time they graduate from high school," he told me. They are well on their way.

» **Karen and John** are married with a 2-year-old child. The good news is that Karen and John had the foresight to set up a college savings plan for their son not long after he was born. The even better news is that now that they have taken steps to fund their son's college education, Karen is expecting their second child (which just so happens to be a girl).

While Karen and John will continue to fund their son's college education fund, they will also have to set something up for their

daughter. John even remarked that they might have to establish some sort of future "wedding" fund, but that's an issue dealt with in the preceding chapter.

For now, as Karen and John's family expands, they intend to continue setting up college education savings plans for each child and fund them to the maximum as best they can on an annual basis. Their hope is that when college comes, it does not create any financial strain on their household because they took the necessary steps and planned ahead.

THREE FINANCIAL STEPS FOR PARENTS

In that regard, there are three steps that you absolutely, positively, without question must take if you decide to adopt or have children:

1. Review your life insurance and make sure you have enough.
2. Update your estate plan.
3. If you haven't already started saving for college, start. As Tyler might say, start saving NOW!

 Life insurance is fairly straightforward. We will cover this topic in greater detail in Chapter 7, but here's a brief synopsis. Once you have/adopt a child, you have now committed yourself to being the financial provider for this little person until they are an adult. As such, it is your responsibility to take the necessary steps to provide for this child in the event that you and/or your spouse are not around to care for them.

What we are concerned about here is income. Namely, how do we replace your income in the event that you are not around? Life insurance provides the most cost-effective solution to the problem of who will provide for little Tommy and Jenny when you and/or your spouse are dead. And yes, I have seen situations where both parents die at the same time and leave their children parentless.

The amount and the type of life insurance (see Chapter 7) is up to you and your spouse. But let me provide you with this one additional piece of advice. I have seen many situations where a parent has died and the spouse, and in some cases a close relative, has come to my office to figure out how to provide for the children. In all of these cases, I have never, ever heard anyone utter the following phrase:

"I wish they hadn't taken out so much life insurance. There is just too much money here."

On the other hand, I've certainly heard the following on more than one occasion:

"I wish there was more life insurance. It's not a lot, but it's all we have to work with, so we'll do the best we can."

My advice is, don't be cheap. Life insurance is one situation where the decision you make today can be felt in your family for generations. It's amazing to think that your decisions can impact your family and future generations in such a profound manner, but they do. I have seen it many times over. The decision to save a few dollars today can cost your family not just the home and their lifestyle in the short term, but more importantly it can wind up costing them their financial future. Spend the extra few dollars and guarantee your family's financial stability and never leave something as important as this to chance just because you wanted to save a buck or two.

PREPAID TUITION PLANS VS. COLLEGE SAVINGS PLANS

There are two types of 529 plans: prepaid tuition and college savings plans. Prepaid tuition plans allow parents to lock in today's college tuition expenses for their children and prepay the future cost of their education today. These programs can be very appealing because of the ability to "lock in" today's prices on a future expense. This type of a plan requires scheduled payments and all investment decisions are handled by the state administrator managing the plan.

The other type of vehicle is a college savings plan. Think of this as a pool of money that comes with no guarantees and can require your input with regards to investment allocation, etc. You can add money to this plan one time or as frequently as you wish. The idea here is that you can save and earn enough money to cover any future college tuition and other expenses by having a large enough pile of money. But be forewarned: There are no guarantees with this type of a plan that you will have saved enough to cover all of your future college expenses.

Most of the financial media talk is about college savings plans, so we'll follow suit.

THE BEAUTY OF 529 COLLEGE SAVINGS PLANS

Four qualities make 529 college savings plans attractive:

» *The income tax benefits can be generous.* Your investment grows tax-deferred, and distributions to pay for the beneficiary's college costs are withdrawn federal tax-free based on current tax law. In addition, you may qualify for additional state income tax benefits if you fund a qualified account using your state's respective 529 plan during the calendar year.

» *The donor (i.e., you) retains control of the account.* With rare exceptions, the named beneficiary has no right of access to the money. You determine when withdrawals are made.

» *They are easy to set up and maintain.* Fill out a simple enrollment form, start making your contributions, and then—*voila!*—the plan is on automatic pilot. The continuing investment of your account is handled by the plan, not you. Or if you prefer, some plans allow that you can mix the asset(s) and determine how you want to allocate your contributions. Plan assets are professionally managed either by the respective state treasurer's office or by an outside investment company. If you decide to shift your investment dollars around, you can chose a different option within the 529 savings program every year, or you can rollover your account to a different state's program, provided no such rollover for your beneficiary has occurred in the previous 12 months. Please note that different state plans may charge different levels for initial investment purchases, ongoing management and administration charges, as well as annual fees and expenses associated with the investment manager. Please read the 529 plan literature so that you understand all the fees and expenses associated with the plan on an annual basis (as some state plans are more expensive than others).

» *Everyone is eligible to participate, regardless of income or situation.* Moreover, investment amount limits are generous, running into several hundreds of thousands of dollars, depending on the state.

Updating your estate plan begins with consulting your estate planning attorney. Since we have not gotten to Chapter 8 yet, I won't give away too much information, except for this: Your will is one of the most important documents you can have in the event you have children. If you and your spouse should die simultaneously in, say, a car accident, you want to have an updated will that spells out who is to be the guardian(s) of your child/children.

Most new parents often neglect to update their estate plan because they have been too busy with interrupted sleep schedules, 3 a.m. trips to the pediatrician and changing diapers to pay attention to the idea of updating estate documents, such as the will. This is one of those mistakes that can impact your family for generations. If there are no named guardian(s) for your children, they are considered to be a ward of the state and the state will decide who is best suited to raise your child. (Please note that each state has different rules regarding the welfare of an orphaned child.)

But to me, the idea of someone else having a say as to who raises my child is simply unacceptable. As a parent, it is your decision and your responsibility to spell out who is to raise your children in the event you and your spouse are not in the picture. So as responsible parents that only want the best for their children, take the necessary steps by calling an estate planning attorney today.

SAVING FOR COLLEGE

The sooner you get started on saving for college, the easier your life will be when they head off to campus many years from now. If you are like me, you read newspapers, magazines and online columns that have always talked about saving for college sooner, rather

" THE COST OF FUNDING YOUR CHILD/CHILDREN'S COLLEGE EDUCATION IS SECOND ONLY TO FUNDING YOUR OWN RETIREMENT. "

than later. The "experts" say that saving today leads to less pain in the pocketbook later.

If you have questions about how to save for college (whether to use a 529 college education savings plan, or a UTMA/UGMA account, etc.) I recommend that you go to Amazon.com or your local bookstore and pick up a few education-funding books. I won't cover these issues in detail here.

The point I'm making is that parents must fund college early, and fund it often. College is an impending liability. It will happen, just like retirement, whether you are prepared for it or not. You can't slow your kids down or hit the "pause" button to give you time to fund their college expenses. Bite the bullet now and save today. As they approach college age, life will be less stressful and more enjoyable because you'll know that you do not have to turn your life upside down to pay the tuition.

TO DO LIST:

1. Review and update your life insurance.
2. Update your estate plan.
3. Start saving for college NOW.

CHAPTER 5

REAL ESTATE: YOUR VERY OWN PIECE OF THE "AMERICAN DREAM"

> "LAND IS THE ONLY THING IN THE WORLD WORTH WORKIN' FOR, WORTH FIGHTIN' FOR, WORTH DYIN' FOR, BECAUSE IT'S THE ONLY THING THAT LASTS."
> — GERALD O'HARA, GONE WITH THE WIND

My very first experience with real estate occurred when I decided to get my own townhouse. I was single, tired of living with roommates and felt that the time had come to have my very own place. More importantly, I was making good money for a single person and Uncle Sam was taking a large piece out of my wallet on an annual basis. It was time for me to leverage my situation and gain an invaluable tax break in the process.

With all of those factors in play, I decided to put down roots in my community and bought my very own place.

GETTING STARTED

The "American Dream" is the idea that you can start with virtually nothing (i.e., graduate from college with little or no net worth), work your way up the corporate ladder and eventually make enough money to buy a home. Owning a home and no longer being a renter is a humongous transformation. That said, mortgage payments can make the monthly rent look like peanuts. For many of us, it's a bit nerve-wracking when the first mortgage payment comes due.

After I got married, my wife and I decided that moving to a larger home was our next big step. Firming our resolve was the fact that in our neighborhood, some jerk keyed my car and, shortly thereafter, another jerk set his van on fire to collect the insurance premiums. It was time to get out!

And thus began the long and exhaustive process of selling our current residence, finding a new one and my least favorite activity, packing and unpacking everything we owned. I almost hate moving as much as I do shopping. Next to getting married, getting divorced or dealing with a death in the family, moving is deemed the most stressful event in life.

Real estate prices in our area at the time had been on an absolute tear. Your standard sales contract now had language in it called an "escalation clause." This meant that prospective buyers would bid their initial price, and then include an escalation clause that says they're willing to go to x amount over the offering price in y increments. This little addendum to the sales contract is absolutely fabulous to those who are selling their homes—and absolute hell for those looking to purchase.

Selling our current residence was a snap in the superheated real estate climate. Indeed, the market was in the midst of a speculative frenzy, unseen since the tulip mania of 17th century Holland. Our Realtor had two open houses on a Saturday and Sunday afternoon while we were out of town. When we came back, we had six sales contracts to review. In the end, we accepted an offer that was higher than our initial asking price. The flip side of this was that we paid an arm and a leg (our opinion) for our new home, which goes to show you that in any financial matter, there is no free lunch.

Today's first-time and even seasoned home buyers are finding the options available to them to finance their piece of the American Dream flexible, extremely complex—and a bit overwhelming. Gone are the days of the straight 30-year, fixed mortgage and the need to put 20% down as a minimum to purchase a home. Today, we have ARMs (adjustable rate mortgages), no money down, negative amortization, interest-only loans and 40-year term loans that can complicate the decision of which mortgage is right for you.

We could spend an entire book on how to get the best loan, where to get it from, and what constitutes a reasonable fee, but that is not the purpose of this chapter. I want to emphasize the idea that real estate ownership is an effective way to leverage cash flow and your ability to purchase a high-dollar asset. Experts agree that real estate also constitutes a strategic part of a balanced investment portfolio. Home ownership is a nice feeling, like mom and apple pie, but it's also a multi-faceted investment tool.

INSIDER NOTES I want to emphasize the idea that real estate ownership is an effective way to leverage cash flow and your ability to purchase a high-dollar asset. Experts agree that real estate also constitutes a strategic part of a balanced investment portfolio. Home ownership is a nice feeling, like mom and apple pie, but it's also a multi-faceted investment tool.

This chapter will also point out related issues you should investigate, such as schools; Realtors who work for their fee and those that don't; traffic commutes; rental real estate; etc.

For starters, find a reliable mortgage banker and settlement attorney you can trust who will work for *you*. Seek out professionals who can explain every step of the process to you, because you are about to commit yourself to hundreds of thousands, if not millions, of dollars in liabilities. With all of that money at stake, you need to completely understand what you are signing. The process of buying and financing a home is complex and number intensive. I strongly urge you to get someone in your corner who will patiently walk you through the process, from start to finish.

Once you have decided to upgrade to a different home and you have settled on the appropriate size and type, there are lots of other considerations when house hunting. Is the neighborhood safe and attractive and does it feature a homeowners association? Are there lots of kids around? What's the quality of the school system? Are there suitable places for kids to play (an issue if you already have kids or intend to have kids)? Where are the closest grocery stores, restaurants, dry cleaners and movie theatres? Are there too many cross streets where commuters cut through at excessive rates of speed? Are there nearby jogging paths, bike trails, parks, soccer fields, baseball diamonds?..You get the idea. Investigate all of these aspects because they will constitute your overall quality of life.

Make a list of what is important to you not only in your potential new dwelling, but also in the neighborhood. I personally like a neighborhood where neighbors can't look in my kitchen or see what I'm watching on television. I like trees and landscaping and I don't really care for street lights that are on all night (I like it dark at night). My wife and I also like to hear the bugs outside our window at night instead of the roar of the big city. Write down what is important to you. What's negotiable and what's not up for debate?

The process of actually moving is probably the most disruptive activity in a household. (One clear benefit: It's an opportunity to weed out a lot of unnecessary crap from your attic, garage and closets.) Have lots of sturdy boxes on hand and label everything. Remember to start early for an orderly and sane packing experience. There's nothing worse than getting rushed and just dumping drawers and closets full of stuff into boxes. Start early, get organized and remember to label all items with a Magic Marker (skip the label maker). You can make the unpacking process easier for yourself and the movers by color-coding boxes, according to the rooms in your new home. For example, the movers will know that the boxes with the yellow stickers on them go into the room with the yellow sticker above the doorframe. That way, you won't be forced, at the most inopportune time, to hunt all over the new home for the box with the toilet paper in it.

If you decide to hire a moving company, you will increase your overall moving costs, but your lower back will thank you.

SECOND HOMES AND RENTAL PROPERTIES

Magazines, newspapers, television, radio and even billboards today are loudly touting real estate. Pitches for easy real estate financing, regardless of credit history or income, bombard consumers day and night. Experts proclaim Americans' undying love of real estate and how "safe" it is compared to stocks, bonds or any other type of investment.

GETTING STARTED

Not too long ago, my wife and I took a cab ride in Las Vegas on our way to a mountain biking trip of the Grand Canyon. The cab driver told us about his recent purchase of a $450,000 condo, overlooking The Strip in a yet-to-be-built community. He said they would not even break ground on the development until fall (we were visiting in late May). I asked him if he intended to rent it. "No way," he said. "I'm buying it for the pure price appreciation. I don't need rental income." I asked him what he would do if no one wanted to buy it. "Never gonna happen," he confidently asserted.

Yeah. Sure. Right. Cab drivers are excellent contrarian indicators—that is, if the average Joe is all hot-and-bothered about a certain investment, it probably means that the market has reached a top and it's about to nosedive. Investors tend to get swept up in the irrational exuberance of crowds. Your job, as an investor, is to remain cool and rational at all times. Never forget one of the laws of physics, as it applies to all investments in general and real estate in particular: what goes up, must *come down (sooner or later).*

Let me recap for those of you not accustomed to financial talk. The cab driver/real estate investor bought a $450,000 condo for pure speculative gain. He has no renter for the property and he has added a fixed monthly obligation by acquiring the mortgage on the condo. Add to this the fact that even though it hasn't even been built yet, he still has to make the monthly mortgage payments on the condo. If the bottom falls out of the real estate market (i.e., no price appreciation) and he can't sell the property at a profit, he is stuck with the monthly mortgage obligation.

But real estate never loses value, right? Wrong. No tree ever grows indefinitely toward the sky. More to the point, the day I get investment tips from a cab driver is the day I need to switch careers.

REAL ESTATE, REAL PEOPLE

» **Chris** is a 29-year-old firefighter who recently purchased his first home, in this case a condo. To afford the down-payment and closing costs, Chris worked a lot of overtime and saved his money by living at home with his parents. After a few minor repairs, new carpeting and some fresh paint, he was able to move into his new home in the spring of 2004.

Chris realized his American Dream of home ownership through years of saving and hard work. While Chris is now in a position at the fire department to afford his own place, he decided to get a roommate to increase his monthly cash flow and to offset some of his monthly expenses.

While the addition of the roommate is not his "ideal" situation, it does allow Chris extra flexibility with regard to cash flow. For now, the roommate is a good fit. But after a few more promotions and salary increases at the fire department, he is already starting to think about upgrading to a larger single family home.

» **Alicia and Allen** got married in June 2003. Previously, each had an apartment rented with roommates. After they tied the knot, they consolidated residences and eventually decided that owning a home made more sense than renting. They bought a house in the community they had been living in for some time.

Alicia was just starting medical school. Both spouses were fully aware of the fact that they probably would not remain in the area for a long period of time. Upon Alicia's completion of medical school, they anticipated relocating for her residency program.

After a thorough discussion and analysis of renting versus buying, Alicia and Allen decided that they would not get the full benefit over the short term from purchasing a home, because the situation would be temporary and they would refrain from fixing up the place. And yet, they determined that home ownership still made more sense than renting for three or four years. Rent payments garnered no equity or tax breaks. Home ownership, on the other hand, conferred equity accumulation and a host of tax deductions, such as for interest payments, state taxes and local real estate taxes.

» **David** is a single guy who bought his first home back in 1995. At that time, David bought into a brand new development that was in an area that had not seen a lot of home building to that point. Over the years, the neighborhood David originally entered has been built up with more communities and amenities. David has considered "locking in" his paper gains by selling his current residence now and using the $250,000 capital gain exclusion as a smart tax move.

To be sure, second homes and vacation properties can make a lot of sense, if you have the cash flow to support them. Real estate is an investment that makes full use of controlled leverage (you will notice I said "controlled") to purchase a property. The advantage of leverage is illustrated in my examples below.

Let's say you purchased a second home five years ago. You bought a $200,000 mountain home and paid 20% down (or $40,000) with a $160,000 mortgage. According to the National Association of Realtors, the median U.S. home price increased in value 55% over the last five years (for more info, consult the NAR's website: www.realtor.org).

While David contemplates selling his current residence, he has taken steps in the interim to increase the value of his current residence. David used some of the equity he had in the home to take out a home equity line of credit and use the proceeds to finish the basement. This process started by David cleaning out and storing the contents of the basement offsite. He performed a good bit of work himself and farmed out home improvement jobs to selected contractors, such as a plumber and an electrician.

The basement project was no small feat and required time, money and hard work. Because this is only David's second time looking for a home to purchase, he has had to learn about "escalation clauses" and how they will greatly help him when he sells his current residence.

So let's assume that the $200,000 home with a 55% increase in value is now worth $310,000. That's a $110,000 gain on a $40,000 down payment, equating to a return on your initial investment of about 275% in only five years.

If you compare a 275% increase in the value of your second home against the Standard & Poor's 500 index during the same time frame, your investment in the second home is the clear winner (the S&P 500 index lost money over the same period).

Don't always assume that your real estate investment will continue to escalate, year after year. Sizzling real estate markets inevitably cool off. Stocks, especially large cap stocks, were invincible from 1995 through early 2000, but I know a lot of folks who are still licking their wounds over their losses after the stock market tanked in 2000.

TO-DO LIST

» Update you cash flow statement.

» Get mortgage projections from a mortgage banker before you make any decisions.

» Find a real estate agent who will work for you and help you through the process.

CHAPTER 6

RETIREMENT PLANNING
-OR- TWO SIX-MONTH VACATIONS EVERY YEAR

> "ONE THOUSAND DOLLARS LEFT TO EARN INTEREST AT 8 PERCENT A YEAR WILL GROW TO $43 QUADRILLION IN 400 YEARS, BUT THE FIRST HUNDRED YEARS ARE THE HARDEST."
> — SIDNEY HOMER, *A HISTORY OF INTEREST RATES*

Retirement is a very simple process when you get down to it. For those of us who are too young to retire, think of retirement as two six-month vacations every year for the rest of your life. Retirement means not having to get up at 5 a.m. during the "work week" to get to the office early to avoid traffic. Retirement means *you* determine when you get out of bed each day of the week and what you do with your day.

For example: You could wake up one morning and decide that you are still sleepy and need an additional three hours in bed. You can go back to sleep until 10 a.m., at which point you get up, pour yourself a big

bowl of Lucky Charms and head out to the golf course, Home Depot, fishing pond or volunteer activity that you enjoy, and spend the rest of the day doing what makes you happy. That is retirement.

It is much different than when you are working because then your calendar, your schedule, almost everything is determined ahead of time for you. During the work week, your alarm clock goes off every morning at the same #!*^$% time. Your boss sets a 9 a.m. Monday management meeting and—*presto!*—your calendar has been scheduled. You'd better be there if you want to keep your job. Kids get out of swimming practice at 4 p.m. and—*presto!*—you need to go pick them up and take them home.

Retirement sounds great, doesn't it? It should. Most people (those of us who are sane) aspire to retire at some point before we are too old and feeble to enjoy it. But to get to retirement, you need a pile of money. That is the key to realizing your retirement. You need a pile of money. The sooner you accumulate your pile of money, the sooner you can retire. One of your greatest sources of leverage is relative youth. Over a long period of time, you can more effectively ride out the ups and downs of the stock market to realize healthy average gains, and you can

INSIDER NOTES The sooner you accumulate your pile of money, the sooner you can retire. One of your greatest sources of leverage is relative youth. Over a long period of time, you can more effectively ride out the ups and downs of the stock market to realize healthy average gains, and you can take better advantage of the magic of compound interest. That's why you should start planning for retirement as soon as possible.

take better advantage of the magic of compound interest. That's why you should start planning for retirement as soon as possible.

One important note: Retirement is different from any other big purchase you will make in your lifetime. You cannot borrow to pay for your retirement. You cannot finance it over 60 months. You either have enough money to retire, or you do not. Period.

Retirement planning isn't too complicated, even though you can't pick up a magazine or newspaper or book that doesn't feature some secret "key" to making your retirement dreams a reality. No, all you need is your own pile of money. Just realize that your pile of money may be bigger or smaller than your neighbor's. The size of your pile of money is purely a function of how early you plan to retire, your life expectancy in retirement, how much you need to live on in retirement, and what kind of annual distribution you'll need from your accumulated retirement fund(s).

This chapter won't delve into the best way to provide your stream of income in retirement, or whether a 4% or 5% distribution factor is an acceptable rate for a retiree, or how you, too, can become a multimillionaire from the comfort of your recliner with no money down.

The good news is that this chapter will highlight certain pre-retirement issues that, as young non-retirees, we all need to know. If we are doing something wrong today and can change our behavior(s), our future retirement situation can be changed for the better. Let's get started.

THE FIVE FUNDING SOURCES

There are five possible funding sources of your retirement:
1. Social Security
2. Employer pensions

3. Personal savings
4. Lottery
5. Inheritance (we'll talk more about this in Chapter 10)

We will spend some time discussing each. Please keep in mind that you may not have all of these sources to work with. My employer does not provide a pension, so I can draw a big red X through "Employer pensions." And an X through Inheritance, because I do not want to assume I will get one. And just for kicks, I like to draw a big red X through Social Security because it just means my pile of money has to be that much larger than my neighbors. How is that for pressure to save?

Let me emphasize that I also do not play the lottery—nor should you—so I can draw another big red X over that source as well. You stand the same chance of winning the lottery as getting hit by lightning—twice! As far as I'm concerned, the lottery is a regressive tax on the naïve. It's unconscionable that state governments, which are supposed to look out for its citizens, market lotteries as retirement solutions. The truly regrettable situation is that those who are least able to afford it tend to be the heaviest spenders on the old American fallacy of getting rich quick. That's why the gambling industry in America racks up $40 billion a year, more than the domestic movie and music industries combined. Instead of gambling in a casino, or spending money on the lottery, I suggest that you simply burn your money in the fireplace—it's a more efficient waste of your cash, and at least you'll heat the room. (I'll say more on the lottery later.)

SOCIAL SECURITY

Disclaimer: This is my common sense assessment of Social Security. Depending upon which political party you listen to, you'll hear different reasons for the problems with Social Security. Understand this: The idiots (yes, they're idiots, regardless of ideological persuasion) on Capitol Hill can barely agree on when to go to the bathroom, let alone agree on what ails Social Security, or how to fix it. But as Americans who pay 12.4% (6.2% employee plus 6.2% employer contribution) of their wages into the system, we need to be aware of the potential impact of any change to the system because it will come right out of our pocketbook.

Social Security in the U.S. provides retirees with a monthly income check for as long as they live. The Iron Chancellor of Germany, Otto von Bismarck, created a similar social security system in 1870 in his country to supply government workers with a small stipend at retirement (and to stave off the proletarian revolutions that were sweeping the European continent). President Franklin D. Roosevelt ushered in the creation of Social Security in one of his "New Deal" packages. The very first recipient of Social Security in the U.S. was Ida May Fuller. She paid into the system approximately $24.75 and received benefits totaling $22,888.92 during her lifetime (Source: Social Security Administration).

In 1950, there were 16 workers paying into Social Security for every one person receiving benefits. Today, there are approximately 3.3 workers paying into Social Security for every one person receiving benefits. Sometime in the next 50 years, due to the Baby Boom generation retiring, this number will fall to two workers paying into the system. Demographic changes will transform the number of workers contributing to Social Security. Add to this the fact that we are living longer, i.e., receiving benefits for a longer period of time, and you get the stark picture of a looming problem.

Moreover, each successive generation of Social Security recipients enjoys higher benefits. That's because benefits are indexed to wages. And if you look at wages over time, they have steadily increased during the past 50 years (see chart).

NATIONAL AVERAGE WAGE INDEXING SERIES, 1951-2004

Year	Index	Year	Index	Year	Index
1951	2,799.16	1971	6,497.08	1991	21,811.60
1952	2,973.32	1972	7,133.80	1992	22,935.42
1953	3,139.44	1973	7,580.16	1993	23,132.67
1954	3,155.64	1974	8,030.76	1994	23,753.53
1955	3,301.44	1975	8,630.92	1995	24,705.66
1956	3,532.36	1976	9,226.48	1996	25,913.90
1957	3,641.72	1977	9,779.44	1997	27,426.00
1958	3,673.80	1978	10,556.03	1998	28,861.44
1959	3,855.80	1979	11,479.46	1999	30,469.84
1960	4,007.12	1980	12,513.46	2000	32,154.82
1961	4,086.76	1981	13,773.10	2001	32,921.92
1962	4,291.40	1982	14,531.34	2002	33,252.09
1963	4,396.64	1983	15,239.24	2003	34,064.95
1964	4,576.32	1984	16,135.07	2004	35,648.55
1965	4,658.72	1985	16,822.51		
1966	4,938.36	1986	17,321.82		
1967	5,213.44	1987	18,426.51		
1968	5,571.76	1988	19,334.04		
1969	5,893.76	1989	20,099.55		
1970	6,186.24	1990	21,027.98		

Source: Social Security Administration, National Average Wage Index.

Today, an average worker can expect Social Security benefits of $14,000 (see chart from AARP, The Social Security Benefit Formula Fact Sheet, August 2003).

RETIREMENT PLANNING

Average Indexed Monthly Earnings (at age 65): $2,438
       90% of first $606   = **$545.40**

32% of the next $607 through $2,438   = **$586.24**
    ($2,438—$606 = $1,832)
    (0.32 x $1,832 = $586.24)

      Primary Insurance Amount   **$1,131.00**
         ($1,131.64 rounded
  to the next lowest dollar = $1,131.00.)

By 2050, an average benefit is projected to be $20,000 in today's dollars. If you do the math, that is a 40% increase over today's average benefit.

So, to recap, in the future, there will be less workers paying into the system, recipients will be receiving approximately 40% higher payouts than they are today, and there will be 76 million more people receiving benefits than there are today. The bottom line: We're screwed. We've promised too much benefit to too many people and we don't have the money to pay for it.

Congress has promised generation after generation of American workers that if you pay into the system, you will receive a Social Security check at retirement. I do not expect Congress to break that promise because the largest voting block of Americans in our society today are retirees (who just so happen to be receiving Social Security benefits). Members of Congress, if they want to keep their day jobs, will be reluctant to decrease Social Security benefits for existing recipi-

ents or increase the taxes they pay on their benefits. Instead, they will turn to those of us still paying into the system and make us responsible for their inability to develop a comprehensive solution to the problem that they created and have refused to fix for generations. Thank you, Congress, for a job well done!

So know this: There will be Social Security in the future. It will simply look different than it does today. Workers will probably have higher payroll taxes (read: less take-home pay), lower Social Security benefits at retirement, higher taxes on Social Security benefits during retirement (ain't that a kick in the head: You pay taxes to fund the system and when you actually receive your benefits, they are taxed again!), and a later retirement age (current full benefits start at age 65, expect it to move to at least age 70). So there you have it.

EMPLOYER PENSIONS

Pensions (a.k.a. defined benefit plans) were very popular many years ago before the advent of the 401(k) plan (defined contribution plan). In the past, workers would go to work for a single company and stay there for 30+ years. The company, wanting to provide for its workforce, would set aside monies in a general account that would be invested on the employees' behalf. When the employee retired, a stream of income (i.e., a pension) could be provided to the employee and/or spouse for as long as they lived.

This is what retirement looked like for my grandparents. They worked for the same organization for over 30 years, and when they retired they each received a gold watch and a pension. The pensions, as well as Social Security, combined to provide grandma and grandpa with a comfortable retirement (you'll notice I said comfortable, not rich).

But this is not what retirement looks like today. First of all, very few employees will stay at a company for their entire working career. Current graduates from college can expect to change jobs multiple times during their lifetime. On top of that, pensions are very expensive liabilities for companies (just ask IBM, United Airlines, Ford and GM—major blue chip corporations that have eliminated or drastically reduced their pension guarantees to workers). Pensions require cash flow to fund on an annual basis, which diverts corporate resources away from more productive uses, such as research and development. So companies with pensions are becoming dinosaurs.

To be sure, some companies still provide their workers with pensions. The federal government is a notable example. If you work for the government for a long enough period of time, you can qualify for a pension. In some cases, these pensions come with a COLA (cost of living adjustment). This means that your pension may increase over time, in an attempt to keep pace with inflation. This is a good thing. Because a pension without a COLA one year may be a good deal, but

INSIDER NOTES Therein lies the big difference between personal savings versus Social Security or employer pensions. With Social Security and pensions, the employer/government sets the money aside and manages the investments, assuming all risk. With personal savings, you are responsible for setting aside dollars and for making the investment decisions. You assume the risk. If you make wise choices and your money does well, you have nothing to worry about. But if you invest all of your personal savings in Uncle Bob's water park and it goes out of business, you might find yourself eating the proverbial cat food in retirement.

> **THE SMARTEST COURSE OF ACTION IS TO ENROLL IN YOUR EMPLOYER'S RETIREMENT PLAN AND FUND IT TO THE MAXIMUM EVERY SINGLE YEAR.**

30 years down the road, when your buying power has been eroded by inflation, the pension may not look like such a good deal.

PERSONAL SAVINGS

The third possible source of retirement income is personal savings. When we say personal savings, think of this as your personal pile of money. You accumulate your pile of money through savings and wise investments over time. Different types of personal savings include: 401(k), 403(b), 457, ESOP and TSP plans; traditional, SIMPLE, SEP and Roth IRAs; brokerage accounts; annuities; and any other investment accounts that you personally fund on an annual basis.

Therein lies the big difference between personal savings versus Social Security or employer pensions. With Social Security and pensions, the employer/government sets the money aside and manages the investments, assuming all risk. With personal savings, you are responsible for setting aside dollars and for making the investment decisions. You assume the risk. If you make wise choices and your money does well, you have nothing to worry about. But if you invest all of your personal savings in Uncle Bob's water park and it goes out of business, you might find yourself eating the proverbial cat food in retirement.

One of the easiest ways to accumulate your pile of money is through the use of your employer's retirement plan. Hopefully your employer cares

REAL RETIREMENT SCENARIOS

CASE STUDY

» **Amy and Robert** have been married for almost 10 years now and are in their mid 30s. They have no children and do not plan to start a family. Robert works for a major pharmaceutical company and Amy works for a marketing firm.

Since both Amy and Robert work full time, they have very good cash flow on a monthly basis. Both feel that saving is very important to them. They learned that lesson the hard way by watching their parents, who did not save as much as they could have. Both max out their 401(k) plans at their jobs and Robert gets stock options, plus the option to buy company stock at a 15% discount of current market price on an annual basis.

Amy and Robert have for a number of years invested sizeable after-tax dollars on a monthly basis into their investments. Both have a long-term perspective of the market and are not overly concerned with short-term swings in value. Their goal is to be able to retire by age 50. To achieve this goal, they are willing to sacrifice a "cushy" current lifestyle today for the promise of an early retirement in the future.

» **Megan and Erik** have been married for a few years and live in North Carolina. They have no children at the moment but do plan to start a family in the near future. Both Megan and Erik are engineers and work full time at high-wage jobs.

Years earlier, when Erik was single, he was making very good money for a recent college graduate, and his father urged him to see an advisor regarding saving and investing. Since Erik was traveling extensively at the time outside of the country, he found he

had a lot of cash on a monthly basis to invest, on top of maxing out his 401(k) plan at his employer. By the time Erik and Megan were married a few years later, Erik had accumulated a sizeable asset base for a single individual.

Unfortunately, not all of Erik's investing experience was positive. Erik got started investing in late 1998 and 1999, and in 2000, the market traded down for three straight years (2000-2002). Erik's initial investments were bought when the market was very high and declined accordingly as the market went south. But Erik was not dismayed and added to his investments. They have since recovered.

Today, Megan and Erik continue to add to both their retirement plans as well as their after-tax investments on a regular basis. They realize they may not be able to maintain their current level of savings when they start their family and one of them goes part-time, but for now they intend to save as much as possible for the future.

» **Maureen and Bill** have been married for five years and live in Virginia. When I first started writing this book in the summer of 2004, they had no children. But lo and behold, in early 2005, Maureen and Bill welcomed their first son into the family.

Maureen is a teacher and Bill works in the medical profession. They have been concerned about saving for retirement for many years. Both Maureen and Bill have qualified retirement plans at their jobs and made sure that they funded these plans to the maximum each year. In addition, Maureen and Bill had accumulated a sizeable amount of after-tax dollars and wanted to invest these for the long term.

A big difference between Maureen and Bill is their investment preferences. Maureen is more accepting of risk than Bill. Maureen and Bill had to find some "middle ground" where each was comfortable with what the other party was investing in, and vice versa.

Another big issue was that Maureen and Bill did not own a house. They had rented for many years and once their son arrived home from the hospital, came to the conclusion that they needed to find a larger home for their growing family.

Since they had been renters for many years, Maureen and Bill did not have much in the way of income-tax deductions on an annual basis. They claimed the standard deduction, instead of being able to itemize if they had a home mortgage. This made them sensitive to paying taxes on an annual basis, especially on their investments. Maureen and Bill make sure that they shelter as much money as possible in tax-deferred investments on an annual basis (read: qualified retirement plans, IRAs, etc.) to keep their tax bill manageable.

enough about its employees to offer a retirement plan of some kind, such as a 401(k). The smartest course of action is to enroll in your employer's retirement plan and fund it to the maximum every single year. Consider this advice the "Golden Rule" for your golden years.

The reasons behind this rule are very compelling:

1. A dollar invested is a dollar invested, which means Uncle Sam doesn't take his grubby paws and take a third out for federal taxes. You could instead pay the taxes on the money and then turn around and invest your after-tax proceeds in another investment, such as a brokerage account or an IRA. But just remember, to make this after-tax investment, you already had Uncle Same take a good-sized

haircut off the top, meaning you're already in the hole and have a lot of ground to make up just to get back to even. Fund the qualified retirement plan first, then if you have leftover dollars, fund another investment account.

2. It lowers your annual tax bill. In 2005 the maximum contribution to a 401(k) plan was $14,000 (if you are over the age of 50 you get an additional catch-up contribution of $4,000 for a total of $18,000). In 2006, the base contribution increased to $15,000, with a maximum catch-up contribution of $5,000. Maximizing your contributions to your employer retirement plan lowers your total tax bill and gives you a rare chance to enjoy an advantage over the IRS.

3. Your investments in a qualified retirement plan grow income-tax deferred. That means you are not taxed on these monies until you take the money out at retirement. It does not mean that you should take a loan out, as you can with some plans, to buy a new Harley or speedboat. Never take a loan from a retirement plan. But it does mean you could be looking at 30, 40 or maybe even 50 years of tax-deferred earnings and appreciation on your original investment. This is a great benefit and I encourage you to take advantage of it as much as possible.

4. Some employers make contributions to employee accounts on an annual basis, such as a percentage of your total compensation. But in most cases, you have to be in it to win it (i.e., you have to already be a contributor to get the employer contribution). Think of this as "free money." You are already setting aside money out of your paycheck on a monthly basis and now your employer adds a little extra.

LOTTERY

I am convinced that America is the greatest place on earth to live. Where else can you walk into a convenience store at 2 a.m. looking for cheesy poofs, a Slurpee, a glazed doughnut and walk out with a chance at winning $150 million? Never mind the fact that your odds of winning are insanely prohibitive. The lottery is for many individuals a hope that they can become an instant millionaire. Winning the lottery will put their dreams on the fast track: "gi-normous" house(s), big fancy cars, designer clothes, expensive jewelry, in essence the MTV *Cribs* lifestyle. (Quick note: Many lottery winners end up bankrupt, with lives ruined by drugs, alcohol, debt and madness, because they couldn't effectively manage their windfall.)

But more to the point, here's the cruel truth of the lottery: Your odds of winning are 1 in 176 million (estimated odds of winning when California joins the Mega Millions lottery, says *USAToday*). The odds of winning the Powerball Lottery are 1 in 121 million.

As I stated earlier, the lottery is a tax on gullible people. Americans love their lottery. They love it so much that they shelled out $48 billion on lotteries in 2004, according to the North American Association of State and Provincial Lotteries. All this lottery money is floating around week after week, and you stand very little chance of seeing any of it (the truth hurts).

INSIDER NOTES Your investments in a qualified retirement plan grow income-tax deferred. That means you are not taxed on these monies until you take the money out at retirement. It does not mean that you should take a loan out, as you can with some plans, to buy a new Harley or speedboat. Never take a loan from a retirement plan. But it does mean you could be looking at 30, 40 or maybe even 50 years of tax-deferred earnings and appreciation on your original investment. This is a great benefit and I encourage you to take advantage of it as much as possible.

GETTING STARTED

What little (if any) benefit you will see from the lottery will not come from your winnings. It will come in the form of better roads, schools and other services from your state government. The Tax Foundation estimated that states made a net $14 billion from lotteries in fiscal year 2003. The lottery allows states to tax the less-educated who, by purchasing lottery tickets, end up paying for state-funded projects. It's akin to a "sin tax" on cigarettes or alcohol. The lotteries are big business, and the one thing I have learned is that when it comes to big business, rarely does the little guy win.

Just ask the state of California. California recently was added to the Mega Millions lottery. California Lottery spokeswoman Cathy Johnson estimated in a *USAToday* article (June 15, 2005) that the new game will bring the state of California as much as $500 million a year in additional revenue (sure beats a tax increase, doesn't it?). This is easy money, taken out of the wallets of hard-working people. Politicians don't have the guts to raise taxes, so they've become addicted to lottery money. It's a scandal.

But do lottery winners really cruise down Easy Street after they strike it rich? Sometimes winning the lottery doesn't necessarily equate to happily ever after. The following stories provide examples of those fortunate enough to win and the aftermath:

» Evelyn Williams won the New Jersey lottery *twice* (1985, 1986) to the tune of $5.4 million. Today, she lives in a trailer and the money is all gone.

» William Post won $16.2 million in the Pennsylvania lottery in 1988 and now gets by on his Social Security check, since all his money was lost to lawsuits and bad investments.

» Janite Lee won $18 million in 1993. According to published reports, eight years after winning, she filed for bankruptcy with only $700 cash in the bank. (Source: Bankrate.com)

LIFESTYLES OF THE BROKE AND CLUELESS

CASE STUDY

A couple, both age 57, came to me for help. They had been married for many years and their son was in his senior year of high school. The husband was the primary bread winner and made over $350,000/year. They had great cash flow from his income, so she did not work outside of the home.

This couple had plans to retire and move to the beach in about 5 years. The problem with this situation became very apparent early in the meeting. They wore designer clothes and expensive jewelry; she drove a brand new Jaguar, he drove a brand new convertible Corvette. And he had two chromed-out Harleys in his garage. They had a huge mansion in an affluent neighborhood and their teenaged son drove a brand new $45,000 Lexus. They had nice toys and took expensive vacations. They spent well. They spent *really* well. Literally everything he made on an annual basis, and then some, was all devoted to their lifestyle.

When we started to talk about income needs in retirement, they figured they could endure a few "hard sacrifices" and make do on about $200,000/year. In my experience with clients, most people have a hard time cutting their income by a third in retirement for the first couple of years. Usually they like to maintain their pre-retirement lifestyle and travel extensively, remodel the home(s), etc. Consequently, I thought this was not a realistic expectation, but we continued to discuss the matter. The main dilemma soon came to light.

He made $350,000 a year and they spent all $350,000 of it during the year. And they saved nothing. Okay, almost nothing. In fact, between both husband and wife, excluding the equity in

the house (which wasn't too much because they kept refinancing and taking out more and more equity to finance their lifestyle), had managed to save between the two of them—and I am not making this up—about $170,000. That's right: $170,000. They had managed to work for the better part of 30 years and had not been able to accumulate more than $170,000, even with income in excess of a quarter of a million dollars per year. And they wanted to retire in five years and "make do" on $200,000 per year.

Now, putting aside his ability to save more than he was making for the next five years, and assuming outrageously positive stock market returns, it does not take a Harvard-educated mathematical genius or a sophisticated retirement calculator to figure out their probability of achieving a successful retirement in five years.

Say it with me now: Z-E-R-O. Nada. Zip. Zilch.

This story serves as a great example to highlight a disturbing fact among a lot of the populace: Most investors don't have a clue about how much they need to save for retirement. And here are the cold hard facts to back this statement up*:
» 32% of investors think they need less than $250,000 in assets.
» 53% of investors think they need less than $500,000 in assets.
» 71% of investors think they need less than $1,000,000 in assets.
» 10% replied and said they were not sure how much they need.

*Source: Employee Benefit Research Institute and Mathew Greenwald & Associates, Inc.

2005 Retirement Confidence Survey.

RETIREMENT PLANNING

FOUR PROVEN RULES

So what do you do? How can you prepare for retirement when retirement is 20 or 30+ years into the future? Follow these four proven rules for retirement success:

RULE #1– Max out your contributions on an annual basis to your qualified retirement plan at work. Save for retirement, cut your tax bill and screw Uncle Sam—all at the same time!

RULE #2– Invest for the long haul. It is not what you make in an "up" market; it's what you don't lose in the "down" market that determines your success (or failure) investing over time. And remember the old saying: Don't confuse a bull market with brains. Most investors tend to do well when the market is hot. The key is to survive the downturns without losing your shirt, so you can ride the upswings.

RULE #3– Consolidate your retirement plans when you change employers. Don't let old 401(k) plans stay behind when you switch jobs (which is always an option). Roll over your 401(k) plan into your new 401(k) plan (if allowed) or to an IRA account. Take control of your financial destiny.

RULE #4– Don't compare your investment returns to your neighbor's. That's a big mistake. Outperforming your neighbors comes down to achieving your goals and objectives. Focus on yourself and your family and stick to your objectives. Your success over the long term will come from achieving your goals over time; your neighbors might fail because they focused on immediate returns. Remember: Retirement planning is a marathon, not a sprint.

GETTING STARTED

TO DO LIST:

1. Fund your qualified retirement plan (401(k), 403(b), 457, TSP, SIMPLE IRA, SEP IRA, Individual 401(k) plan, Keogh, profit-sharing plan, etc.) to the maximum every year!

2. Make sure you designate a primary and contingent beneficiary for your qualified retirement plans, IRAs, Roth IRAs and your life insurance.

3. Save now. The earlier you start, the easier it is later in life. Choose to save your hard-earned money now, versus spending it on a fancy lifestyle. You will reap the fruits of your sacrifices later in retirement.

CHAPTER 7

RISK MANAGEMENT: PROTECTING YOURSELF

> "TROUBLE IS ONLY OPPORTUNITY IN WORK CLOTHES."
> — HENRY KAISER, INDUSTRIALIST AND THE FATHER OF MODERN SHIPBUILDING

Accidents happen and always at the worst possible time. You must not only protect your family from financial catastrophe, but you also need to procure the right insurance for the right circumstances. Insurance isn't just a necessary evil; it's also an investment that requires careful planning and analysis. Making the wrong choices can reverberate for generations.

Risk is defined by Webster's as "the chance of injury, damage, or loss; dangerous chance; hazard." For purposes of our discussion, think of risk as the chance of suffering a financial loss. Risk is everywhere and in everything that you do on a daily basis. Getting in your car and driving to work (someone could run a red light and T-bone your car)

❝ WITH ANY INSURANCE CONTRACT, IT'S IMPORTANT TO READ THE FINE PRINT. THERE'S OFTEN A CHASM BETWEEN WHAT THE SALESPERSON PROMISED YOU, AND WHAT THE INSURANCE CARRIER ACTUALLY OWES YOU WHEN THE CHIPS ARE DOWN. ❞

and eating out at your favorite restaurant (your waiter/waitress could steal your credit card and use it fraudulently), to shopping at the grocery store (you could slip on a grape and break your back, forcing you to miss work for several months) are everyday risks that we do not think about. You must take the necessary preventive steps to protect yourself, your family and your assets at all times.

The issue here isn't only about mitigating risk. By ensuring basic financial security for the people and things that you cherish most, you will have more leeway to be growth-oriented with your other investments.

The following is a partial list of different types of insurance coverage we need/should be familiar with:
» Personal Liability
» Life
» Disability
» Automobile
» Homeowners
» Special Rider

PERSONAL LIABILITY INSURANCE

It's probably the single most important type of insurance coverage every person should have, yet so few actually do. Personal liability coverage is a necessity in today's litigious society.

READER: Excuse me? Are you insinuating that we Americans are litigious?

AUTHOR: Yes, I am.

READER: That upsets me greatly. I'm going to sue you for reckless emotional distress.

AUTHOR: Go ahead. Make my day.

Here is my rationale for this comment. Turn on your TV, open any newspaper or magazine and you will be bombarded with ads from attorneys looking to "help you." Sue your employer because you were laid off or fired for no (good) reason. Sue the doctor who misdiagnosed a medical condition. Sue your child's coach because your kid didn't make the football or pep squad. Don't like your neighbors' 20-foot-tall inflatable Santa Claus in their front yard until April? Sue on the grounds it causes you severe emotional distress. Thought the neighbor-

INSIDER NOTES If a jury awards damages to someone stemming from an act of your negligence, you may be covered by basic limits of liability insurance provided through both your homeowner's and/or automobile insurance policies. Take a moment to dig up your policy cover page and examine the limits listed on each policy.

hood fast food restaurant's drive-thru coffee was too hot? Sue because coffee should never be *that* hot. Don't like the fact that your town doesn't recognize Festivus (for the rest of us) as a holiday? Sue the town council and claim exclusionary religious preferences.

Sue who? Sue everybody.

Now, some of these are probably valid reasons and some of them are not. I can understand suing your neighbor because they let their pitbull out and it ate your child. That makes sense to me. I can also understand suing a motorist who clips your back bumper because he/she is tailgating. I can also understand suing your employer for a work-related injury. But suing because your kid didn't make the baseball team since he/she is not the next Roger Clemens or because your cup of coffee is too hot? Suck it up and get over it.

But that's the problem. Some people can't get over it. And they are more than willing to be nasty about it and go to great lengths to make their feelings known. This is the type of person you have to watch for and protect yourself from. We're a society of angry people who feel alienated from one another. Seemingly everyone has a chip on his shoulder. Hassles that were once sorted out on an individual basis now end up in court. Civility and a sense of community are increasingly relics of the past.

Enter liability insurance.

According to a big name insurance company's website, "If you accidentally injure someone or damage their property, you could be the person being sued." The key term here is "accidentally." This is called negligence. If you accidentally sideswipe a vehicle on a major highway while trying to change lanes, this could be classified as negligence. You did not intend to hit the car, it was simply an accident. Having a bad case of road rage and being upset with the other car's driver and wanting to teach someone a lesson would not qualify as negligence.

If a jury awards damages to someone stemming from an act of your negligence, you may be covered by basic limits of liability insurance provided through both your homeowner's and/or automobile insurance policies. Take a moment to dig up your policy cover page and examine the limits listed on each policy.

Let's say you sideswipe a car on your way home from work while trying to change lanes, all while on your cell phone. The car you inevitably hit will more than likely be more expensive than your car. This is called Murphy's Law. In addition, the driver of said vehicle is the chief of surgery at the regional hospital. Oops. Now you're really in trouble. First you damage his BMW and now there is the possibility that he may have been injured and unable to work for a few weeks or months. Odds are pretty good that he intends to sue you for damages since you caused the accident and injuries.

INSIDER NOTES Not all liability coverage adds an additional $1 million to your basic liability on your homeowner's or automobile insurance policy. Your particular insurance carrier may have a different method for calculating your total coverage. Make sure you understand your carrier's specific contract language now, rather than setting yourself up for a surprise later. Please note that state rules may vary liability protection on an individual level. Consult your insurance agent or nearest 1-800 number for full information and details.

Other types of accidents that may/may not be your fault but for which you can still be found liable: UPS delivery person slips and falls on your icy walk because you didn't de-ice the path, and she breaks her back; your dog gets out and bites a child who just happens to be walking home from school; teenagers decide to hop the 5-foot-tall fence surrounding your covered pool for a late-night dip, and one of them drowns underneath the pool cover in the process; your teenage driver, while attempting to changes lanes, talk on a cell phone *and* change the song on his iPod knocks a motorcyclist off his bike and into a ditch, sustaining head and back injuries in addition to destroying his prized Harley-Davidson Road King.

Let's assume your automobile policy has liability coverage of $100,000 per person with a cap of $300,000 per accident. In English, this means the most the insurance company will cover is up to $100,000 per person in an accident. If the doctor sues you for $500,000 and the jury sides with the good doctor, the insurance company says, "It has been great doing business with you, here's our $100,000. Have a nice day."

READER: But the total bill is $500,000. You only gave me $100,000?!

INSURANCE COMPANY: We covered you to the maximum liability limit per our agreed-upon insurance contract.

READER: But who will make up the $400,000 difference?

(Dead silence.)

The answer is you get stuck with the difference. This is an instance where your home, your retirement assets, even your wages could be taken, sold or garnished because of a) your mistake and b) your lack of substantial liability coverage to protect yourself, your family and your assets. Your decision to carry the basic amount of liability insurance coverage means that you assume any and all risk associated with an accident in which you are found to be negligent. If the court awards for the plaintiff an amount that exceeds your basic coverage, you're in trouble.

But everyone makes mistakes. The key is to carry a personal liability policy to protect you from mistakes because if you live long enough you and/or your spouse will make a mistake. A personal liability policy is designed so that if a claim above your basic liability coverage on either your automobile (or homeowner's) policy is put to you, you have an additional layer of liability protection. Liability policies are sold in increments of $1 million up to $5 million and thereafter in $5 million increments (typically). It may be possible to insure yourself and/or your spouse plus any immediate family members up to several million dollars. Note: It may also be possible to increase the base liability coverage on an individual automobile and homeowner's insurance policy.

Let's go back to the accident where you hit the doctor and are sued for $500,000. The court finds for the doctor and you are ordered to pay $500,000. Your basic automobile coverage limit is $100,000, but because you have a personal liability policy (that has been integrated

INSIDER NOTES Remember this fundamental premise: Life insurance equals income replacement for those who are still working (read: pre-retirement). While you are a working member of society, your dependent children at home can't go out and replace you and/or your spouse's income. They also may not have sufficient assets to provide for the family, in the event of your or your spouse's death. Life insurance provides protection from this short-term need.

> ## "THERE IS ALSO A HIDDEN PSYCHOLOGICAL BOOST FROM THE SUDDEN INFLUX OF INSURANCE PROCEEDS: COMFORT. "

with your automobile and homeowner's policies) for $1 million. The insurance company would pick up the entire cost of defending you and the judgment against you. In this case, a personal liability policy would put the insurance company on the hook for not only the basic $100,000 of automobile liability, but an additional $1 million.

Not all liability coverage adds $1 million to your basic liability on your homeowner's or automobile insurance policy. Your particular insurance carrier may have a different method for calculating your total coverage. Make sure you understand your carrier's specific contract language now, rather than setting yourself up for a surprise later. Please note that state rules may vary liability protection on an individual level. Consult your insurance agent or nearest 1-800 number for full information and details.

With any insurance contract, it's important to read the fine print. There's often a chasm between what the salesperson promised you and what the insurance carrier actually owes you when the chips are down.

In today's litigious society, everyone should have a personal liability policy that is integrated with both your homeowner's and automobile insurance policies. To not have this type of insurance coverage is one of the single biggest financial risks any person can assume. To assume this type of risk is, for lack of a better word, stupid. The cost on such policies can range from a several hundred dollars to several thousand dollars (and up), depending on the coverage limit, your carrier and your situation.

Rule of thumb: If you have substantial assets (read: more than a $5 million net worth), you should absolutely, positively, without a reasonable doubt have a sizeable umbrella liability policy. It's simple: The more you have, the more you have at risk from unscrupulous people who will take advantage of your situation when possible. Protect yourself and your assets. The same goes for the rest of us who do not have a $5 million estate. Make sure you have an integrated umbrella liability policy. No exceptions!

Please note that if you have a history of speeding tickets, accidents, maybe even a D.U.I., obtaining this type of a policy may be somewhat of a challenge and may be cost prohibitive. Have a teenager in the house that drives? Keep a pitbull in the backyard? Own a pool, Jet Ski or other personal watercraft? These types of situations also can make acquiring this type of a policy slightly more expensive. It may not be cheap, but then again, the alternative of not having this additional coverage is not a pretty picture, either.

LIFE INSURANCE

Let's face it: Death is an unpleasant subject that most of us push to the back of our minds. Human beings don't like to ponder their mortality. It's no surprise, then, that even though people are quick to insure their material possessions, they're often reluctant to insure their most valuable asset of all—their lives. That's a big mistake that can incur dire consequences for your loved ones (see sidebar Page 128, "Unhappy Ending").

Remember this fundamental premise: life insurance equals income replacement for those who are still working (read: pre-retirement).

While you are a working member of society, your dependent children at home can't go out and replace your or your spouse's income. They also may not have sufficient assets to provide for the family, in the event of your and/or your spouse's death. Life insurance provides protection from this short-term need.

Now there are many different types of life insurance (term, whole life, universal life, variable universal life, etc.). But we're not worried about what type of insurance you have. What we are concerned with is making sure that you and/or your family members (i.e., those you leave behind) are protected from financial ruin in the event you are not around to provide for them.

READER: But I'm not married and I have no dependents.

AUTHOR: Then I would argue that your life insurance needs are minimal at best—unless you want to leave your parents a gift for having put up with your butt for all those years, or you want to endow a scholarship at your college, or make a sizeable gift to a charity you feel very strongly about.

READER: Awesome. But what happens when I get married?

AUTHOR: Your needs have probably changed. Better discuss this with your spouse.

READER: And what happens if we have children?

AUTHOR: Your needs just changed again. I'd argue you absolutely need to increase your life insurance now.

READER: So every time I experience a life-changing event—marriage, divorce, accumulation of one child or more—my life insurance needs may change?

AUTHOR: Bingo!

Maintaining life insurance policies can provide you and/or your heirs with added flexibility that is not present if they terminate their life insurance coverage. Life insurance proceeds at death provide instant liquidity at a time when expenses can be heavy and out of place (funeral costs).

There is also a hidden psychological boost from the sudden influx of insurance proceeds: comfort. To those who have recently lost a loved one, money should be the last thing on their mind. But for some strange reason, it is one of the very first things people think about. Questions such as "How will I survive? How will I buy groceries or pay the mortgage?" can overwhelm the most sophisticated of individuals. A large infusion of insurance proceeds can provide that needed "safety blanket" at a time when clients are caught in a time of grief, anxiety and depression.

If the worst should happen and your spouse should die prematurely, what should you do with the proceeds? Pay off the mortgage? Invest it

INSIDER NOTES Uninsured motorist coverage covers you in the event you are struck by someone with no automobile insurance or a hit-and-run driver. Underinsured motorist coverage pays in the event the driver who hit you causes more damage than his/her insurance policy can cover. Please note that in some states both of these coverages may pay for property damage.

all? Go to Las Vegas and bet everything on red 37? What is the best strategy? The answer is that it depends upon your specific situation. But if you are depending on the insurance proceeds as "income replacement," then you consult professional legal, tax and investment counsel for help in managing your new situation.

Do not be afraid to ask for help in this type of a situation. Your primary focus at this difficult time should be yourself and your family. Find someone you can trust to help you with the finances only after you and your family have had time to grieve. Never rush to make a financial decision in the heat of the moment or during a time like this. That's how mistakes happen. Park the proceeds at your bank and leave it alone. It will be there in a few months when you've got a clear head and have had time to adjust to your situation.

There is another school of thought that says life insurance is eventually not needed because there is a nest egg that has accumulated and even if something happened to the client or spouse, the insurance proceeds are superfluous. The transfer of household cash flow to life insurance premiums may not be the best use of premium dollars for some clients. But this decision should be based on how comfortable you, or more importantly, how your spouse feels about terminating the coverage.

Be careful going down this road. I have heard a lot of widows and widowers wish that their spouse had more life insurance coverage at their death, but I have yet to hear someone complain that their spouse had too much coverage.

Just remember that life insurance is very fluid. Your life insurance needs will change as you go through life—e.g., add a spouse, add a child or two or three, lose a spouse, retire, etc. Your life insurance needs will need to be constantly re-evaluated to make sure you have the

RISK MANAGEMENT

INSURANCE SCENARIOS IN THE REAL WORLD

CASE STUDY

» **Alison and Jim** are married with two children, ages 13 and 11. He works for a major telecommunications company and she is a stay-at-home mom. They recently relocated to Florida for Jim's job, but hope that the assignment is temporary as he moves up through the company.

Alison's and Jim's life insurance situation was like a lot of individuals. All of Jim's life insurance was through his employer. In the event that Jim lost his job, all of his life insurance coverage would have been left at his previous employer. Alison and Jim felt that this may not the best way to protect the family against the risk of Jim's premature death.

Instead of maintaining the employer life insurance policy, Alison and Jim considered options through independent term life insurance companies. A 20-year term policy with a face value of $1.5 million was selected to cover the short-term income replacement needs of the household. The policy term was long enough to fund Jim and April's retirement and to see both boys through college.

The independent life insurance policy was portable, so if Jim ever left his job, his family was protected against his premature death. In addition, it turned out that the policy cost less on an annual basis than a similar policy through his employer. Alison and Jim also obtained an insurance policy for Alison, something they hadn't done before. They reasoned that her duties as a mother and homemaker were no less important than Jim's daily activities on the job.

» **Amy** is a registered nurse (RN) at the local hospital. She works in the cardiac/telemetry unit, a step down in severity from the Intensive Care Unit (ICU). The patients she sees on a daily basis are very sick and require a lot of "assistance." This assistance usually takes the form of strenuous physical exertion on Amy's part.

The National Institute of Occupational Safety and Health (OSHA) says that a "51-pound stable object with handles is the maximum amount" anyone should "routinely lift." Amy and most other nurses will tell you that they routinely lift people at the hospital that are much heavier than 51 pounds, and none of them have handles (unless maybe you count "love handles").

Because of the heavy lifting of patients, day in and day out, studies have shown that nurses overall have a 40% higher probability of suffering a non-fatal occupational injury than the general public. That is a huge risk to Amy and her spouse.

For protection against job-related injuries, Amy opted to enroll in the short-term and long-term disability coverage offered through her employer. While the coverage is adequate (read: will pay monthly benefits up to 60% of her most recent paycheck prior to the accident), it does decrease her bottom-line, take-home pay on a monthly basis. But to Amy, 60% of her paycheck is better than nothing at all.

» **Rachel and Adam** are married with two children, ages 4 and 2. Adam works as an engineer and Rachel is primarily a stay-at-home mom. They recently purchased a new home, which afforded them more space for the kids to play and a backyard.

Since Adam is the primary breadwinner in the house, a review of their balance sheet and income needs determined that there was not enough coverage on Adam if something happened to him. Adam acquired a "two-times salary" life insurance policy through his employer, and a separate $250,000 term life policy through an independent insurance company.

Rachel and Adam were smart to acquire a separate insurance policy outside of the employer's benefits, but they both agreed that an increase in the overall coverage for Adam also would be a prudent course of action.

However, another issue was the lack of coverage on Rachel, which meant that Adam would be at a significant disadvantage should he need help to run the household if Rachel were not around. Consequently, Rachel and Adam took the prudent step of obtaining coverage on Rachel, albeit at a smaller amount of coverage than Adam.

INSURANCE TO-DO LIST:

1. Pull policy face pages for homeowner's/renter's/condo, automobile, special rider, disability and personal liability policies and make sure the coverage levels are adequate and up to date.
2. Examine all financial ratings of insurance companies you do business with.
3. Make a detailed inventory of all "the stuff" in the house. Keep receipts of high-priced ticket items, electronics, etc. Keep all inventory, pictures and/or video proof for insurance documentation purposes in a fireproof safe or safety deposit box.

> **I HAVE HEARD A LOT OF WIDOWS AND WIDOWERS WISH THAT THEIR SPOUSE HAD MORE LIFE INSURANCE COVERAGE AT THEIR DEATH, BUT I HAVE YET TO HEAR SOMEONE COMPLAIN THAT THEIR SPOUSE HAD TOO MUCH COVERAGE.**

proper level of coverage. If you have questions or you are not sure your coverage is adequate, then seek professional assistance.

Just an observation: I have noticed a distinct difference between people who are financially savvy and have a high net worth and those who are average investors and do not have a high net worth. A person's financial insurability is the total amount of life insurance for which they can qualify. For most people, this is approximately the size of their net worth (total assets minus total liabilities equals net worth).

Most average investors typically consider their insurability only when purchasing life insurance to provide income replacement for their spouse and/or family. This is a good start, but financially savvy, large net-worth investors take it to the next level. They understand that life insurance can be used to significantly boost their net worth—or rather, their family's net worth—at their death.

Most financial publications tell investors to buy the minimal amount of life insurance for the lowest possible cost. I think this solution can solve a short-term need. But the long-term needs in this situation are possibly being ignored. This can become a situation where you get what you pay for, or rather your family's security is not as good as it could be because you chose the most cost-effective solution on the table.

DISABILITY INSURANCE

According to the 2003 National Underwriter Field Guide, "Individuals between ages 30 and 50 have a 36-47 percent chance of experiencing at least one long-term disability (lasting 90 days or longer) before age 65." Another insurance industry survey indicated that for every home lost because the owner died, another 16 were lost because the owner became disabled.

Disability insurance is probably one of the most commonly overlooked forms of insurance. While life insurance can be financially devastating to a family, the loss of a wage earner due to a disability is in some respects more financially devastating than the actual loss of a spouse. A disability creates a situation where the family's ability to accumulate retirement assets as well as to operate the household on a day-to-day basis is severely impaired because of the reduced cash flow.

With the premature death of the spouse, life insurance proceeds provide an immediate offset against the lost wages of the deceased spouse. With disability, the disabled spouse is still a member of the household. However, ability to earn an income can be limited. In addition, it is possible for a disabled member to have higher medical insurance costs, whereas if they were deceased these would no longer be an issue. The

INSIDER NOTES It's important to make a complete and thorough inventory of everything that you own, whether you own a home or condo, or rent. Obtain pictures, receipts and actual videos of all possessions, from kitchen utensils to stereo equipment to golf clubs to the washer-dryer. If your home is robbed or burns to the ground, you'll have documentation to provide to the insurance company.

ability of a family to save for retirement is impacted because it is more than likely that the disabled spouse is unable to continue to work a normal work week based on the current disability.

Disability insurance is typically acquired through your employer. Employers have the option of offering their employees several different types of disability insurance coverage. There are typically two types of disability insurance coverage; short-term disability and long-term disability.

Short-term disability is typically insurance coverage that begins to pay after a relatively short period of time. Short-term disability coverage can pay benefits from a couple of months to usually up to a two- or three-year period. The benefit is a function of the type of policy. Typically, short-term disability is based on a percentage of your most current paycheck stub. It would probably be most helpful to pull out the original employer's handbook. When you sign on with your employer, examine the type of coverage that they offer.

Long-term disability coverage typically begins after a longer elimination period. This period of time could range from six months to a couple of years and can pay benefits until age 65 or longer. Long-term disability coverage is usually acquired through an individual's employer.

If your current employer does not offer short-term or long-term disability insurance coverage of any type, you should consider the addition of an independent disability policy on your own. While this coverage can be expensive to obtain by an individual, these types of policies can be acquired through professional organizations, clubs and other affiliated organizations.